The Cub Book

Published by Scouts Canada

catalogue #20-202

ISBN: 1-894187-14-8

Welcome To Wolf Cubs!

Dear Wolf Cub,

Welcome to the Wolf Cub pack. Your time here will be filled with fun and adventure. Along the way, you will learn to do a lot of exciting and important things.

Maybe:

You'll go to camp and on outings.
You'll learn how to keep warm,
    make shelters, and cook outdoors.
You'll visit all kinds of interesting places.
You'll learn how to take care of yourself.
You'll plan and do things with your six and pack.
You'll learn about Mowgli, Bagheera,
    Baloo, and the Jungle story.
You'll make gadgets, play games, and
    sing around a campfire.

And, you'll make a whole lot of friends.

This book is written to help you do all these things. It is full of ideas and, if you use it well, it will become like a friend. You can use your book as a diary of the things you did as a Cub and keep it for the rest of your life.

Have Fun and Good Hunting!

Akela
The Old Wolf

The Cub Book
Table of Contents

INTRODUCTION

Wolf Cub

Activity Areas

Introducing the Wolf Cub Activity Areas

Your Cub Book is filled with all sorts of fun activities for you to try. These activities are grouped into six different areas. As you read about each Activity Area, you will see how the activities tie together to make a great Wolf Cub program just for you.

Here is what you'll find in each Activity Area.

The Natural World Activity Area

Explore and learn the secrets of nature. You'll soon discover why all life needs food, water, shelter and space. People are part of the natural world and play an important part in keeping the environment clean and healthy. There are some great ideas on how to help endangered species, parks and even wildlife that live in your own backyard. Taking care of the environment is an important part of your everyday life.

The Outdoor Activity Area

The outdoors is one of the best places for you to learn how to take care of yourselves and others. You'll learn about camping, hiking, cooking, fishing, canoeing and lots of other outdoor skills. Most of all, you will learn how to do these safely while still having lots of fun.

The Creative Expression Activity Area

Being able to work on a special project, either by yourself, with friends or family can be exciting. You'll find lots of activities which involve inventing, building, singing, taking pictures, working a computer, or just coming up with new ideas no one has ever thought of.

The Health and Fitness Activity Area

Learning how to stay fit and healthy is an important part of becoming a grown-up. It's much more fun doing activities when you are in great shape. You won't tire as fast, and you'll be able to play longer. These activities will also show you how smoking, drugs, and alcohol can really hurt you. By keeping healthy, you can do more of the activities you like to do, such as skating, biking, swimming or just doing things with friends.

The Home and Community Activity Area

Helping out at home or in your community is a big responsibility. These activities will show you how to keep your home safe and in good repair. Also, you'll find out about all the different services your community has and how to use them. Learning first aid and how disabled people use community services are valuable home and community skills.

Canada and the World Activity Area

These activities will help you learn about other people, their cultures and religions, and how lucky we all are to be living in a free country. You might even get to explore what it might be like to live in space. Above all, these activities will show you that all people, no matter where they live and who they are, need and depend on one another to have happy, peaceful lives.

An Overview of the Activity Areas

Natural World

Black Star

Badges

Astronomer
Gardener
Naturalist
Observer
Recycling
World Conservation

Award

Canadian Wilderness

Outdoor Activities

 Green Star

Badges

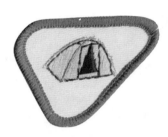

Camping
Cooking
Fishing
Hiking
Trailcraft
Watercraft
Winter Cubbing

Awards

Canadian Camper
Canadian Heritage Trails

Creative Expression

Tawny Star

Badges

Artist
Carpenter
Collector
Computer
Entertainer
Handicraft
Musician
Photographer
Reader

Award

Canadian Arts

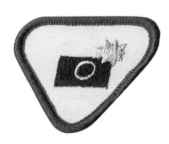

Health and Fitness

 Red Star

Badges

Athlete
Cyclist
Skater
Skier
Snowboarder
Swimmer
Team Player

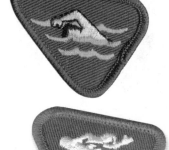

 **Award**

Canadian Healthy Living

Home and Community

 Blue Star

Badges

Disability Awareness
Family Helper
Family Safety
First Aider
Guide
Home Repair
Law Awareness
Pet Care

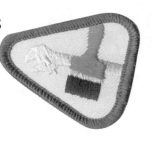

Award

Canadian Family Care

Canada and the World

Purple Star

Badges

Aboriginal Awareness
Canadian Heritage
International Trade
Language Strip
Religion in Life
Space Exploration
World Cubbing
World Religions

Award

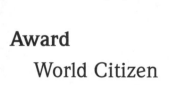

World Citizen

Specialty Badges

Badges

Individual Specialty
Pack Specialty

CHAPTER 1

Wolf Cubs in the Jungle

hy are you and your friends called Wolf Cubs? The idea comes from *The Jungle Book*, by Rudyard Kipling. It's a book of stories about the adventures of Mowgli and the wolf cubs.

Mowgli was a young boy who lived in a village in India. One night, a tiger named Shere Khan attacked some villagers around a woodsman's fire and Mowgli escaped into the jungle. Mowgli found a family of wolves living in a cave, crawled in, and soon curled up with the wolf cubs.

Raksha, the mother wolf, liked the little boy. She wanted the other wolves to let her adopt him, but Shere Khan demanded that the wolves give him Mowgli to eat. Raksha was ready to fight to keep Mowgli as her son. Then Bagheera, the black panther, and Baloo, the wise old bear, persuaded Akela, the chief of the wolf pack, to let Mowgli become a member of the pack.

Mowgli grew up with the wolves. Akela and the other old wolves, along with Bagheera and Baloo taught Mowgli how to live in the jungle and hunt with the pack. With their help, he became wise in jungle lore.

In a real pack, the old wolves take very good care of the cubs. Just like puppies, wolf cubs are very playful and like to jump and run and tumble all the time. The old wolves teach them how to find food and shelter and look after themselves.

Most important, the old wolves teach the cubs how to work together. Wolves hardly ever hunt by themselves. Instead, the wolf pack hunts as a team. When they catch their food, they share it with each other.

The old wolves in your Cub pack have jungle names like Akela, Baloo and Bagheera. They will help you learn how to look after yourself and other people, too.

When I joined the pack, my leaders had these jungle names.

Leader's Name

Jungle Name (Akela, Baloo, Raksha, etc.)

_____   _____

_____   _____

_____   _____

_____   _____

Your leaders may even help you pretend to be the animals found in *The Jungle Book*. You can be Bagheera, the black panther, quietly stalking his prey until he pounces with a ROAR. Ask Akela or one of the other Cubs to show you how.

Some songs, plays and jungle dances I did as a Cub:

_____

_____

_____

_____

_____

_____

Here's a picture of a jungle character I really like.

This is what I learned about my favourite *Jungle Book* character:

_____

_____

_____

_____

Word Search

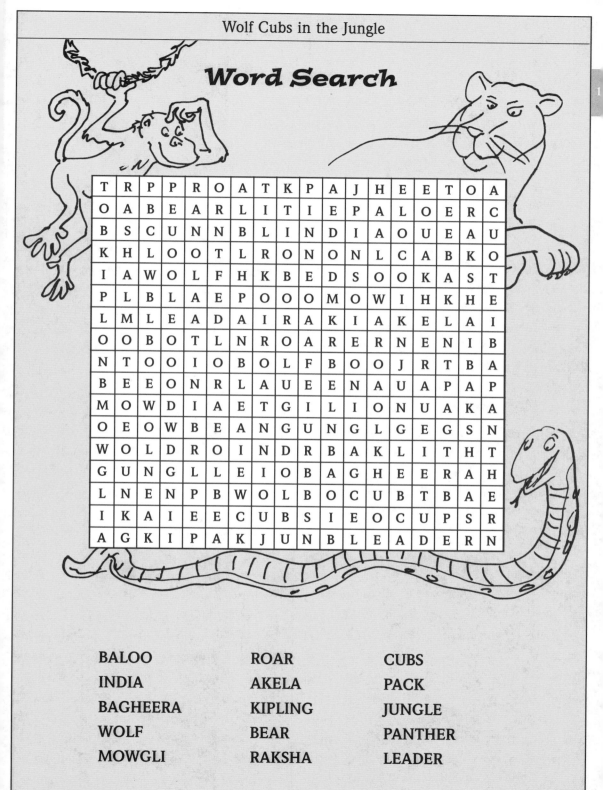

T	R	P	P	R	O	A	T	K	P	A	J	H	E	E	T	O	A
O	A	B	E	A	R	L	I	T	I	E	P	A	L	O	E	R	C
B	S	C	U	N	N	B	L	I	N	D	I	A	O	U	E	A	U
K	H	L	O	O	T	L	R	O	N	O	N	L	C	A	B	K	O
I	A	W	O	L	F	H	K	B	E	D	S	O	O	K	A	S	T
P	L	B	L	A	E	P	O	O	O	M	O	W	I	H	K	H	E
L	M	L	E	A	D	A	I	R	A	K	I	A	K	E	L	A	I
O	O	B	O	T	L	N	R	O	A	R	E	R	N	E	N	I	B
N	T	O	O	I	O	B	O	L	F	B	O	O	J	R	T	B	A
B	E	E	O	N	R	L	A	U	E	E	N	A	U	A	P	A	P
M	O	W	D	I	A	E	T	G	I	L	I	O	N	U	A	K	A
O	E	O	W	B	E	A	N	G	U	N	G	L	G	E	G	S	N
W	O	L	D	R	O	I	N	D	R	B	A	K	L	I	T	H	T
G	U	N	G	L	L	E	I	O	B	A	G	H	E	E	R	A	H
L	N	E	N	P	B	W	O	L	B	O	C	U	B	T	B	A	E
I	K	A	I	E	E	C	U	B	S	I	E	O	C	U	P	S	R
A	G	K	I	P	A	K	J	U	N	B	L	E	A	D	E	R	N

BALOO	ROAR	CUBS
INDIA	AKELA	PACK
BAGHEERA	KIPLING	JUNGLE
WOLF	BEAR	PANTHER
MOWGLI	RAKSHA	LEADER

19

CHAPTER 2

How to Become a Wolf Cub

W hen you came to your first Cub meeting, your leaders may have welcomed you as a "Tenderpad". The name "Tenderpad" refers to the soft skin on the bottom of a real wolf cub's feet. The older wolves help the Tenderpads learn about the pack, and while they learn, the Tenderpad's feet grow tough. By the time Tenderpads have learned how to work together as a team, their feet have become tough enough to follow the Wolf pack on adventures.

As a Tenderpad, you will be given a pack neckerchief, (Cubs call a scarf a "neckerchief") at your first Cub meeting to wear with your new Cub uniform. The neckerchief is to identify and welcome you as a new pack member. Your next step as a Tenderpad is to learn about being a Wolf Cub. The leaders and older Cubs will help you. If you remember to always do your best while you learn, then soon your feet will grow tough. You will then be able to run not only with the pack, but also on your own adventures.

Here are the things you need to learn to become a Wolf Cub.

CHECK OFF WHEN COMPLETED AND WRITE THE DATE.

_____ ☐ 1. Repeat and explain the Wolf Cub Promise and Law.

_____ ☐ 2. Perform the Grand Howl with other Cubs.

_____ ☐ 3. Demonstrate the Cub salute and handshake, and repeat the Cub motto.

_____ ☐ 4. Read or listen to the story of Lord Baden-Powell.

I completed my Tenderpad requirements on:

_____
(date)

Tenderpad Requirement No. 1

Repeat and explain the Wolf Cub Promise and Wolf Cub Law.

This is the Wolf Cub Promise

1. I promise to do my best,

2. To love and serve God,

3. To do my duty to the Queen;

4. To keep the law of the Wolf Cub Pack;

5. And to do a good turn for somebody every day.

I promise to do my best.

When you promise to do something, it means you will try your hardest to keep your word. Doing your best also means that, when you are doing something important like helping someone with a job or playing a game, you will not give up if it gets tough. You'll stick with it as best you can. Sometimes you may make a mistake. That just means you will try even harder the next time and keep on doing your best every day.

These are some of the promises I made while I was a Tenderpad:

To love and serve God.

While there are many different faiths and ways to worship God, all faiths teach the importance of love, caring and respect for others. When you can take the words of your own faith and put them into daily practice, you are showing how to love and serve God.

These are some of the things I do to live up to the teachings and duties of my own religion:

_____

_____

_____

To do my duty to the Queen.

When you belong to a group like a family, a pack or a country, you need to follow certain rules that help people live and get along together.

Queen Elizabeth is our Queen and the laws of Canada are made in her name. The Queen represents our country and all its people, and the crown she wears is the symbol of authority. We do our duty to the Queen and our country by obeying the law.

When we obey the traffic safety laws and respect other people's property, we are doing our duty to the Queen and all Canadians. Whenever we do something to help make Canada a better country, like protecting our environment and helping others, we are also doing our duty to the Queen.

The Governor General is the Chief Scout in Canada and represents the Queen in this country. Who is the Governor General today? _____

The Lieutenant Governor represents the Governor General in your province. Who is the Lieutenant Governor in your province today? _____

The Commissioner represents the Governor General in the Territories. If you live in a Territory, who is your Commissioner today? _____

To keep the Law of the Wolf Cub Pack.

The Law of the Wolf Cub Pack says:

The Cub respects the Old Wolf;
The Cub respects himself/herself.

When Mowgli lived with the wolves in the jungle, he learned that they had to hunt together and follow the directions of Akela, the Old Wolf, if they were going to survive. Just as the Queen represents the people and the country of Canada, the Old Wolf represents the Cubs and the pack. Obeying the law helps the pack stay together and have fun.

Imagine what your pack would be like if Cubs did just what they felt like doing. There would be lots of noise and running around, but not much else. You wouldn't get a chance to do neat things like going on hikes, camping, crafts and finding out what teamwork is all about.

That's why, in your Cub pack and in a real wolf pack, all the Cubs and young wolves need to do their share to follow the Old Wolf and listen to what he or she says. When you do your share, you are respecting Akela, the Old Wolf, and helping the pack stay together and have fun doing things.

2

Laws or rules are meant to make things better for your whole pack. Sometimes you may feel that a pack law is not quite right or that there is a better way to do something. Because your ideas are important, try to suggest a way to make a law or a rule better. You can do this by talking about your suggestion with Akela or the other Cubs in your six. After the pack has heard your suggestion, do your best to respect and follow its decision, even if it decides not to change things. Respect is very important when you belong to a group like a Cub pack.

If you want to know more about laws, read about the Law Awareness Badge.

And to do a good turn for somebody every day.

Doing a good turn means helping someone just for the sake of helping, without expecting a reward. A good turn can be a big one like saving someone's life, or a small one like smiling at someone or doing the dishes without being asked. Usually, we only have chances to do small good turns, but we have lots of chances to do them because there are so many good turns that need to be done.

When we do a good turn, even a small one, we are also loving and serving God and doing our duty to the Queen, because we are helping to make the world a better place and Canada a better country.

Here are some good turns I've done that I'd like to remember:

_____

_____

_____

Tenderpad Requirement No. 2

Perform the Grand Howl with other Cubs.

Just as Mowgli and the wolves gathered around the council rock to howl a welcome to Akela, the Old Wolf, the Cubs in your pack form a circle and do the Grand Howl to welcome your Akela. Here is what they howl:

"A-h-h K-a-y L-a-a
W-e-e-l-l d-o-o o-o-u-u-r BEST!
D-Y-Y-Y-B, D-Y-Y-Y-B, D-Y-Y-Y-B, D-Y-Y-Y-B
(draw this out like a wolf howl)
W-e-e-l-l DOB, DOB, DOB, DOB!"
(make it sound like short, sharp barks)

DYB (pronounced "dib") means Do Your Best, and
We'll DOB, DOB, DOB, DOB means
we'll Do Our Best.

Akela, another leader, or your sixer will show you how to squat for the Grand Howl, when to jump up, and how to hold your hands.

While you're still a Tenderpad, you will be included in doing the Grand Howl, although you will need a chance to practise it with the other Tenderpads first. When you are invested as a Wolf Cub, you'll receive a Grand Howl in your honour.

This is how loud I howled on the day I was invested.

Circle ONE: **whispered**

spoke

shouted

yelled

**howled so loud
I couldn't hear
anyone else.**

Tenderpad Requirement No. 3

Demonstrate the Wolf Cub salute and Wolf Cub handshake, and repeat the Wolf Cub motto.

Wolf Cub Salute: The salute is a very old form of greeting. Long ago when people greeted each other, they held up their right hand with the palm forward to show that they had no weapon in it. The salute is also a sign of respect and friendship for a leader or another Cub or Scout.

When you salute a leader or another Cub, you use a special sign. You hold your right hand to your head with two fingers spread out to look like the pointed ears of a wolf. Akela will show you how to do it.

Wolf Cub Handshake: Lord Baden-Powell, the founder of Cubbing and Scouting, once met an African chief who greeted him by shaking hands with the left hand. The chief explained that the left handshake was a sign of trust. Why? Because people used to hold their shield in the left hand and had to put it down before they could shake with that hand.

Today, in cultures where it is acceptable, Cubs and Scouts shake hands with the left hand. It is a sign that they are all members of the worldwide Scouting family.

Wolf Cub Motto: The Wolf Cub motto is *"Do Your Best"*. It reminds us that we have promised to do our best always, according to our own personal abilities. In Cubs, winning and losing does not matter. The personal effort you put into trying new things is what really counts.

Tenderpad Requirement No. 4

**Read or listen to the story of Lord Baden-Powell
and how he started Cubbing and Scouting.**

You can read Lord Baden-Powell's story in Chapter 3.
Ask one of your leaders to tell you about some of the
other events in the history of Canadian Scouting.

Tell Akela, your six or your pack some of the
things you have learned about Baden-Powell and how
Cubbing started.

These are some of the things I talked about:

_____

_____

_____

_____

_____

_____

_____

Your Investiture as a Wolf Cub

When you have done the four Tenderpad requirements, Akela will invest you as a Wolf Cub. He or she will ask you to repeat the Wolf Cub promise while the other Cubs make the Cub salute. When you have said the promise, Akela will welcome you as a Wolf Cub and give you your Cub epaulettes.

I was invested on _____ *by Akela, whose*
                              (date)

name is _____ .

This is what I remember about my investiture:

_____

_____

_____

_____

The Wolf Cub Uniform

Your uniform is an important part of Cubbing. Wearing it is your way of telling yourself and other Cubs that you are a Wolf Cub. It also tells people in your community that you are a member of a Wolf Cub pack.

Every time you put on your uniform, remind yourself of your Cub promise and what Cubbing means to you. That way, putting on your uniform helps you prepare yourself to do your best. Take care of your uniform to keep it looking smart so that wearing it will help you feel smart, too.

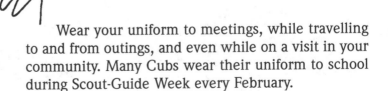

Wear your uniform to meetings, while travelling to and from outings, and even while on a visit in your community. Many Cubs wear their uniform to school during Scout-Guide Week every February.

At times, when you are on a hot summer outing, doing a grimy job, or camping, you will wear other clothes, but there are always many other chances to wear your uniform with pride.

Cub Uniform Chart

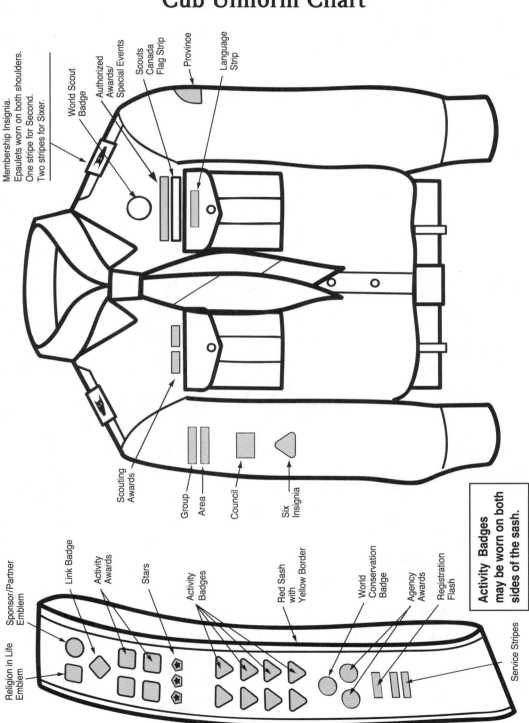

Wolf Cub Section Membership Insignia. Epaulets worn on both shoulders. One stripe for Second. Two stripes for Sixer.

World Scout Badge

Authorized Awards/ Special Events

Scouts Canada Flag Strip

Province

Language Strip

Scouting Awards

Group

Area

Council

Six Insignia

Religion in Life Emblem

Sponsor/Partner Emblem

Link Badge

Activity Awards

Stars

Activity Badges

Red Sash with Yellow Border

World Conservation Badge

Agency Awards

Registration Flash

Service Stripes

Activity Badges may be worn on both sides of the sash.

CHAPTER 3

How Scouting and Cubbing Began

 ord Robert Baden-Powell, called B.-P. for short, started Scouting in Britain in 1907. From his experience as a General in the British army, B.-P. had discovered that children could be trusted to do important jobs once they had been shown what to do. B.-P. had written a book for adults about camping and survival and called it *Aids to Scouting*. In 1907, he decided to write a similar book about Scouting just for children. It was an instant success! Scouting became so popular, that by 1916 he had to write a second book for younger children who wanted to join Scouting. B.-P. called this second book, *The Wolf Cub's Handbook*. The Cub Handbook was based on Rudyard Kipling's *The Jungle Book*. And so Wolf Cubs started.

3

Canadian Cubs have since played an important part in history. During the First and Second World Wars, Cubs helped to collect tons of scrap material for war victims. In peace time, Cubs used their training to help others through community service projects. Every year, Cubs use their first aid training to help injured friends and even save lives.

Cubs also protect the environment. Since 1973, thousands of Cubs have helped plant 3 million trees a year in Canada as part of the Scoutrees for Canada program. In 2002, Scouts Canada celebrated the planting of its 70 millionth tree.

Today, there are over 25 million Scouts worldwide in 216 countries. Thanks to Baden-Powell, his idea of using Scouting to promote world peace and understanding is continuing with your help.

In 2002, Scouts Canada celebrated the planting of its 70 millionth tree.

CHAPTER 4

The Natural World

Activity Area

B.-P. always said that one of the most interesting things you can do is explore the world. You don't even have to travel to a far country. B.-P. taught us that the best and easiest way to explore is to keep our eyes and ears open and notice what's going on around us.

Look at those tracks in the snow. Where do they come from? Where do they go? What kind of animals made them?

Listen to the rain splashing in the puddles. How much rain is going to fall today?

Look at the seeds spinning down like helicopters. What kinds of plants are there to be found?

There are so many things to see, hear, smell and touch.

Do you want to explore your natural world? Here are some things you can do right in your own neighbourhood.

Black Star Activities

If you are interested in learning about nature, here's a good place to start. The Black Star Activities will introduce you to the natural world and how it works.

To earn the Black Star, choose and do any five of the A requirements and any two of the B requirements. These activities can be done by yourself, or with your six, pack, family or friends.

A Requirements

CHECK OFF WHEN COMPLETED AND WRITE THE DATE.

_____ ☐ 1. Care for a lawn or garden for a month.

_____ ☐ 2. Without harming nature, mount and label a display of natural things, such as leaves, weeds, rocks, or seeds and tell about your collection.

_____ ☐ 3. Grow a plant indoors and describe how it grew.

_____ ☐ 4. Grow a sugar or salt crystal on a string.

_____ ☐ 5. Plant a tree or shrub, describe how trees grow and why they are important to nature.

_____ ☐ 6. Point out or describe some sources of pollution in your neighbourhood and describe possible solutions.

_____ ☐ 7. Make a rain gauge and use it to record rain or snowfall for a month.

_____ ☐ 8. Make and set up a bird bath, bird house, or bird feeding station, and look after it for a season.

_____ ☐ 9. Show how to use and take care of common garden tools.

_____ ☐ 10. Using the water cycle, show the route water takes to your home or show how acid rain is formed and how it affects nature.

_____ ☐ 11. Point out the North Star and three constellations.

B Requirements

CHECK OFF WHEN COMPLETED AND WRITE THE DATE.

_____ ☐ 1. Visit a natural area of your choice and point out some different ways the local plants and animals depend on one another for life.

_____ ☐ 2. Go on a ramble and identify six different kinds of birds, or keep a record of birds using a bird bath or bird feeder for a season. Know which birds are protected in your area.

_____ ☐ 3. Visit one of the following places: conservation area, weather station, fish hatchery, observatory, tree farm, fire ranger tower, farm, greenhouse, park, zoo, forestry station, dam. Learn about how this place helps the environment.

I completed my Black Star requirements on:

Robin

_____
(date)

Cedar
Waxwing

Black-capped
Chickadee

Great
Horned Owl

American
Goldfinch

Find out the colour of these birds. Have you seen any of them this year? Where?

Badge Activities

If you enjoy exploring the natural world, and want to discover more about it, here are additional challenging activities you might like to try. These activities can be done by yourself, or with your six, pack, family or friends.

Astronomer Badge

CHECK OFF WHEN COMPLETED AND WRITE THE DATE.

_____ ☐ 1. Teach another Cub how to use the pointer stars of the Big Dipper to find Polaris, the North Star.

_____ ☐ 2. Show how to orient and read a seasonal star map. Be able to find five constellations of your choice.

_____ ☐ 3. Learn and tell a story related to a constellation or an aboriginal legend regarding the night sky.

_____ ☐ 4. Know and describe 3 sky features:
a) Milky Way
b) Aurora Borealis or Northern Lights
c) Comets
d) Meteors
e) Planets
f) Stars
g) Satellites
h) Eclipses

_____ ☐ 5. Know the phases of the moon and the moon's role in causing ocean tides.

I completed my Astronomer Badge requirements on:

_____
(date)

Gardener Badge

CHECK OFF WHEN COMPLETED AND WRITE THE DATE.

_____ ☐ 1. Show the proper use of a spade, fork, hoe, trowel and how to care for them.

_____ ☐ 2. Prepare, plant and look after for three months, one of the following:
   a) A garden at least 1.5 square metres in size
   b) A window box at least
      60 cm x 25 cm in size
   c) Two or more perennial plants in pots
   d) A plant terrarium

Oct. 17 ☑ 3. Identify and name from life any three of the following:
   (a) Six garden flowers
   (b) Six garden vegetables
   c) Four common weeds
   (d) Three common friends of the garden
   e) Three common pests of the garden

Oct 17 ☑ 4. Choose and do any two of the following:
   (a) Grow a bulb.
   (b) Grow a tree seed.
   c) Start a vegetable from seed on blotter paper or paper towelling.
   d) Grow a plant from seedlings.
   e) Grow a plant from the tops of turnips, carrots, radishes, parsnips or beets.

I completed my Gardener Badge requirements on:

_____
   (date)

Naturalist Badge

CHECK OFF WHEN COMPLETED AND WRITE THE DATE.

Do any six of the following:

_____ ☐ 1. Find different kinds of seeds that travel by "helicopter", "parachute", "sling shot", as a "hitchhiker", or by "animal express". Discuss how seeds are dispersed.

_____ ☐ 2. With the help of an adult, dye a piece of cloth or T-shirt using plants to make the colour.

_2010_ ☑ 3. Make a plaster cast or take a picture of an animal track.

_____ ☐ 4. Show at least three different ways animals camouflage themselves.

_____ ☐ 5. Show at least three different ways animals survive the Canadian winter.

_____ ☐ 6. Show at least three examples of how plants and animals protect themselves from weather or predators.

_____ ☐ 7. Take a hike through an urban community to look for nature.

_____ ☐ 8. Observe any wild animal and report on what you learned from its behaviour.

_____ ☐ 9. Find examples in books or real life and tell how plants and animals attract or repel others using colour and smell.

_____ ☐ 10. Describe or draw some ways animals capture or eat food.

I completed my Naturalist Badge requirements on:

_____
(date)

Observer Badge

CHECK OFF WHEN COMPLETED AND WRITE THE DATE.

Do any five of the following:

_____ ☐ 1. Recognize, point out (from life rather than a book where possible), and describe some of the habits of six animals.

_____ ☐ 2. Recognize, point out (from life where possible), and describe some of the habits of six birds.

_____ ☐ 3. Recognize and imitate three bird calls.

_____ ☐ 4. Recognize and point out from life six spring, six summer, or six autumn wild flowers.

_____ ☐ 5. Recognize, observe and report the habits of six insects.

_____ ☐ 6. Recognize and point out from life six trees or shrubs and describe some of their uses.

_____ ☐ 7. Recognize and point out four features of the night sky such as stars, constellations, planets, etc.

_____ ☐ 8. Describe the signs for different types of weather.

_____ ☐ 9. Recognize and point out six different kinds of rocks or minerals.

_____ ☐ 10. Recognize four different animal tracks or animal signs.

I completed my Observer Badge requirements on:

_____

(date)

Recycling Badge

CHECK OFF WHEN COMPLETED AND WRITE THE DATE.

Do any three in each of the categories.

A. Reduce

Feb. 9 ☑ 1. Look in your home or in a store for products that could be sold with less packaging.

_____ ☐ 2. With the help of an adult, check the tire pressure in a car to see if the tires are properly inflated to improve gas consumption.

Nov. 11 ☑ 3. Bring your own non-disposable mug and eating utensils to use at camp or bring a garbage-free lunch to school regularly.

_____ ☐ 4. Make a list or draw how you and your family could reduce the amount of electricity used at home. For one week keep track of how you saved energy. Record what you did and how many times you did it.

_____ ☐ 5. Keep a record of four different ways that you saved water at your house in a week.

_____ ☐ 6. Describe what you and your family did to reduce the amount of heat needed to keep your house warm.

_____ ☐ 7. Choose two items that you or your family bought this week that you could have done without. Commit to not buying those items for the next month.

B. Reuse

_____ ☐ 1. Choose something that you currently throw away and come up with a new idea on how to reuse it safely.

_____ ☐ 2. Explain and show new uses for old plastic containers.

_____ ☐ 3. Explain and show new uses for old jars and cans.

Aug. 20 ☑ 4. Make a project from old lumber or Christmas trees.

_____ ☐ 5. Describe and show new uses for different kinds of paper, greeting cards, bags and cardboard boxes.

_____ ☐ 6. Repair and donate old toys to somebody.

Dec. 2010 ☑ 7. With help from an adult, collect old clothes, furniture or books and donate them.

_____ ☐ 8. Make a list of all the things that you didn't need to buy during one week because you reused items you already had. Explain how reusing items reduces the amount of energy needed to make new things.

C. Recycle

_____ ☐ 1. Build a composter and either use it yourself or give it to a friend.

_____ ☐ 2. Help publicize a home toxic waste collection day in your community, such as for collecting old paints, garden chemicals, oil, etc.

_____ ☐ 3. Show or tell your pack about three products that are made with recycled materials. Explain how using recycled materials helps to reduce climate change.

_____ ☐ 4. Participate in a recycling project such as a bottle or paper drive.

_____ ☐ 5. Visit or learn about a company or industry that is involved in recycling or collecting recyclable materials.

Feb. 9 ☑ 6. Make a list of products that display the recycling symbol.

_____ ☐ 7. Using old paper products, make your own recycled paper.

_____ ☐ 8. Help organize or participate in a recycling program.

_____ ☐ 9. Learn which items in your house can be returned when you are done with them (examples include computer parts, batteries, tires etc.). Identify one item (from this list) you were planning to throw out and with an adult, bring it somewhere to be recycled.

I completed my Recycling Badge requirements on:

_____

(date)

(See page 259)

World Conservation Badge

CHECK OFF WHEN COMPLETED AND WRITE THE DATE.

Do any six of the following:

_____ ☐ 1. Go on a hike in or around two different habitats
such as a field, marsh, bog, woodlands, seashore,
prairie or tundra. In each habitat discover the
following:
   a) What animals live there.
   b) What kinds of plants live there.
   c) What the ground or soil is like.
   d) What the sources of water are for this area.
   e) Explain how if the temperature got hotter or
      colder than usual because of climate change
      the habitat might change.
   Compare the two habitats and discuss why
   some plants and animals live in one place and not
   the other.

_____ ☐ 2. Visit a habitat and discover what kinds of plants
and animals are there that provide food for other
animals. How does food encourage or limit what
animals live in the area?

_____ ☐ 3. Visit a habitat and discover what kinds of animal and
insect homes are there. Discuss the advantages and
disadvantages of each kind of home you find.

_____ ☐ 4. Visit a habitat and look for signs of water. How
does water affect where and what kinds of plants
and animals live there?

_____ ☐ 5. Find out what it means to be an endangered
species. Choose one endangered species and make
a poster or a presentation to your pack on how
it has been hurt by a lack of food, water, shelter,
space or other causes. What can people do to help
this endangered species survive? How could

changes in the average temperature because of climate change make it more difficult for this species to survive?

□ 6. Do a project that improves food, water, shelter or space for wildlife. Some ideas are:
   a) build and install bird houses or feeders
   b) clean up a stream or creek
   c) plant trees or shrubs that have fruit for animals to eat
   d) remove trash or stop erosion so more plants and animals can use the area

□ 7. Discuss the different kinds of soil, water and air pollution that exist. How do these forms of pollution affect your health and the environment, and what can be done to stop or limit pollution sources?

□ 8. Write some rules for good behaviour while in the outdoors and share these with your six or pack.

□ 9. Explain how climate change affects the natural environment and take one action, such as using a bike instead of a car, using less electricity at home or recycling, that will reduce greenhouse gas emissions which cause climate change.

I completed my World Conservation Badge requirements on:

_____
(date)

CLIMATE CHANGE CHALLENGE
DÉFI CHANGEMENT CLIMATIQUE

(See page 259)

Canadian Wilderness Award

Do you want to discover as much as you can about the natural world? Would you like to share your knowledge with other Cubs? If so, you can try earning this award. You'll find these activities both challenging and rewarding to work on. These activities can be done by yourself, or with your six, pack, family or friends.

CHECK OFF WHEN COMPLETED AND WRITE THE DATE.

To achieve this award, you must complete the following:

_____ ☐ 1. Earn the Black Star.

_____ ☐ 2. Earn the World Conservation Badge.

_____ ☐ 3. Earn one other Natural World related badge.

_____ ☐ 4. Learn about and, if possible, visit a Provincial or National Park or Wilderness Area. Create a report or display that highlights the reasons why the park is there and some problems facing the park.

_____ ☐ 5. Participate in a conservation project which improves a local park, sanctuary, refuge or other wilderness area.

_____ ☐ 6. Help show other Cubs some aspect of nature study of your choice.

I completed my Canadian Wilderness Award requirements on:

_____

(date)

This Award may be worn on your Scout sash after you become a Scout.

What All Plants and Animals Need To Survive

Think what it would be like to have to live in the wild. In order to survive, you would need four basic things: food, water, shelter and space. Food is what you would need to keep your body in good shape. Food would also help to keep you warm in the winter. Water is necessary for helping circulate food through your body and getting rid of waste. Water is also useful for keeping you from overheating in the summer. A shelter is your home. Wind, snow and other kinds of weather can be very harmful unless there is some protection. Space is having enough room to grow and live. A small flower may need only a few centimetres to grow, while a grizzly bear needs several hundred kilometres of land.

If you were to lose one of these four basic elements, your ability to survive for very long would quickly disappear. This happens to some wild plants and animals every day in Canada and around the world. When the place where an animal or plant lives, called a "habitat", is carelessly destroyed, it loses its food, water, shelter and space. When a plant

or animal can no longer survive to the point where there are almost none left, they are called "endangered species". If nothing is done to help them survive, they could disappear altogether. When the plant or animal no longer lives anywhere on earth, they are called "extinct".

In Canada, there are about 190 endangered plants and animals that need help to survive. Ask your leaders or family to help you find out about one of them, and talk about what can be done to save them.

The endangered species I found out about was:

_____

_____

_____

How people can help this species survive:

_____

_____

_____

_____

If you would like to learn more about helping Canada's and the world's endangered species, you can write to:

The World Wildlife Fund
245 Eglinton Avenue E.
Suite 410
Toronto, ON
M4P 3J1
www.wwf.org

Or check out the following web sites:
www.cwf-fcf.org (The Canadian Wildlife Federation)
www.cosepac.gc.ca (COSEWIC, Commitee on the Status of Endangered Wildlife in Canada)

Making a Plaster Cast of Animal Tracks

Make a cast of an animal track.

You need:

- a small box or bag of plaster of Paris
- a mixing bowl
- a stick for stirring
- a water bottle with water
- a few cardboard strips.

Plaster of Paris, also called patching plaster, can be found in most hardware stores. For a mixing bowl, use a flexible plastic dish, such as a clean margarine container. After you're finished you don't have to wash it out. Just let the plaster harden, then crack it out by squeezing the dish.

When you have found a track, put a 2 cm high cardboard strip around it like a collar. An easy way to make the collar is to cut a milk carton into 2 cm wide rings. The collar will keep the plaster from running all over the ground.

You'll have to experiment with how much plaster different size tracks will need. For the average dog track, start by putting 10 teaspoons of plaster in the mixing bowl. Slowly add water and stir until the plaster looks like grey pancake batter or cake mix. Carefully pour the plaster into the track and let it harden. You can also practise by making a track in playdough and pouring plaster into the track.

Once the plaster is set, you can lift the cast off the track. Brush off any dirt and you'll see what the foot of the animal that made the track looked like. Notice the shape, where the toes are, and any claw marks. Can you identify what animal made the track?

Nature in the City

Mention the word "city", and you can imagine concrete towers, asphalt highways and smog. While this might not be a quiet forest, finding nature in a city can be as easy as walking down a sidewalk.

Buildings often use local kinds of stone for both strength and beauty. Limestone blocks display fossils of ancient coral reefs, while granite has crystals from when the rock first cooled. You can also find stone from other countries, such as polished marble from Italy.

Trees are very important to cities. They clean the air, shade homes, provide nesting places for wildlife, and help block out noise. Also, many trees look and even smell good, which improves city living. See how many trees you can identify around a city block.

Cities are filled with wildlife, if you watch for it. Squirrels, gophers and woodchucks live in the green strips between busy highways. Deer, skunks, raccoons and even bats find homes in city parks and gardens. Cemeteries offer shelter to many birds and wildlife. Bridges become nest sites for swallows. Even peregrine falcons use skyscrapers as substitute cliffs for raising a family.

Indoor gardens, museums and zoos provide a chance to see plants and animals from around the world.

If you use your Cub eyes, you really can find nature in the "concrete jungle" called cities!

A Nature Collection

Do you like to collect things? Do you have sets of hockey and baseball cards? How about making a nature collection? It's easy and fun, too!

Before you start your collection, there are a few things to think about.

First, some things in nature are very rare, and it is wrong to take them from where they belong. In many provinces, it's even against the law to pick certain flowers. If you're not sure whether you should collect something from nature, leave it where it is. There are lots of other things you can collect instead.

Second, it's not much good to collect a bunch of things if you are just going to pile them up in your room and forget about them. Decide what things you want to collect, then plan how you are going to display them. If you need to, ask someone to help you with a few ideas.

If you collect leaves, dry them thoroughly by pressing them in newspaper under a pile of books, then tape them in a scrap book. If you collect rocks or shells, you can clean off the dirt with an old tooth-brush and mount them in egg cartons.

If you collect seeds, let them dry for about four weeks and glue them to a piece of cardboard.

Make a label for everything you collect to say what it is and where and when you found it. If you don't know what it is, leave that space blank until you find out.

There are books in your school or public library to help you find the names of almost everything under the sun. The librarian or your parents, teacher, or Cub leader can help you. Once you've got your collection well started, show it to your six, your pack, and your leaders.

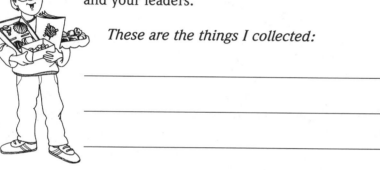

These are the things I collected:

_____

_____

_____

Here is a picture of my collection or something in it that I really liked.

Grow a Garden

You can be a gardener even if you live in a high-rise apartment.

1. Get a few pea, bean or corn seeds.
2. Roll up a piece of blotter or paper towel and put it snugly inside a glass or small bottle. You can buy blotting paper at a stationery or office supply store. If you can't find a blotter, use enough layers of paper towel to make the roll stiff.
3. Fill the glass or bottle about one-quarter full of sawdust or earth.
4. Place your seeds between the blotter and the inside of the glass, above the level of the sawdust.
5. Wet the sawdust or earth enough so that the blotter soaks up the water. If you're using paper towel, pour in the water carefully so that it doesn't get too wet and collapse.
6. Put your glass or bottle in a dark place for a few days. Keep the blotter or towel damp.
7. When the plant starts growing, bring it out into the light again. Keep the blotter or towel damp.

The types of seeds I tried were:

_____

_____

_____

_____

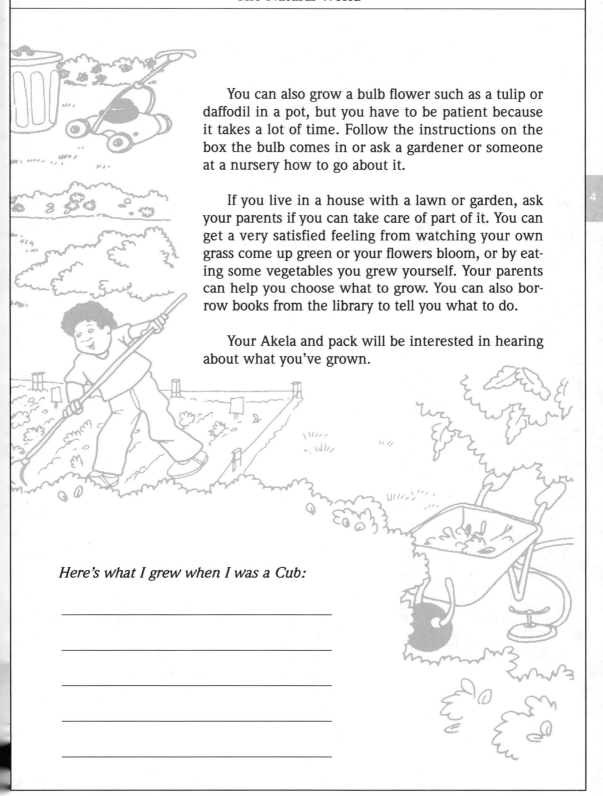

You can also grow a bulb flower such as a tulip or daffodil in a pot, but you have to be patient because it takes a lot of time. Follow the instructions on the box the bulb comes in or ask a gardener or someone at a nursery how to go about it.

If you live in a house with a lawn or garden, ask your parents if you can take care of part of it. You can get a very satisfied feeling from watching your own grass come up green or your flowers bloom, or by eating some vegetables you grew yourself. Your parents can help you choose what to grow. You can also borrow books from the library to tell you what to do.

Your Akela and pack will be interested in hearing about what you've grown.

4

Here's what I grew when I was a Cub:

_____

_____

_____

_____

Making Salt Crystals

Try this experiment to make beautiful crystals out of salt and hot water.

You need:

- a small saucepan
- 250 ml water
- 56 - 75 ml salt, or more
- a clear drinking glass or jar
- a long pencil
- a piece of cotton string
- metal paper clip.

1. Boil the water in the saucepan, and turn off the heat.

2. While stirring, <u>slowly</u> add the salt, a spoonful at a time.

3. If all the salt dissolves, add a little more and keep stirring until no more salt will dissolve and is starting to gather at the bottom of the pot. This is known as a supersaturated solution.

4. When the solution has cooled, pour it into the drinking glass or jar taking care not to transfer any undissolved salt.

5. Tie one end of the string around the pencil and attach the paper clip to the other. Drop the paper clip into the solution making sure it doesn't touch anywhere. Rest the pencil on the rim of the glass.

6. Put the glass in a place where it will stay cool and undisturbed. (You must not touch it or lift it up!)

7. Within 24 hours you will start to see crystals forming on the paper clip and string.

8. Use a magnifying glass to see the cubical crystal shapes.

Measuring Rainfall

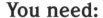

Some days it storms and rains very hard for an hour or so. On other days, the rain comes down gently, but it keeps on falling all day. Which kind of rainfall produces more rain?

You can find out if you make a rain gauge.

You need:

1. A tin can as wide as you can find.

2. A flat place away from trees or walls on which to set the can for collecting rain. The best place to put it is about 30 cm above the ground on a platform.

3. A tall glass jar with straight sides as narrow as you can find. An olive jar is good.

4. A ruler.

5. A grease pencil or a bit of paint and a fine brush.

How to make it:

1. Carefully pour 2 cm of water into the wide tin can.

2. Pour the water from the can into the narrow bottle. Notice how much higher it rises in the bottle.

3. Mark the water level in the bottle with the grease pencil or paint brush. This is the mark for 2 cm of rain.

4. Using the ruler and grease pencil or brush, carefully divide the space between this mark and the bottom of the bottle into 10 equal parts. Each of these marks represents 1/10 of 2 cm, or 2 mm of rainfall. Using the same spacing, mark off the space above the 2 cm line as well.

How to use your rain gauge:

1. Place your can on the flat space before the rain begins.

2. When the rain is over, make sure your bottle is empty, and then pour the water from the can into the bottle and read the rainfall in mm from the marks on the bottle.

Even better, you can keep a continuous record of rainfall by leaving your can in its flat place and, at the same time every day, measuring the amount of rain you find in it. Keep a record for a week or even a month by marking your figures on the calendar or in a notebook. Some days you may find the water level drops. Where do you think the water goes?

Ask your parents or leaders to help you test your rain water's pH level. The pH level will tell you if rain is acid or not. Acid rain is the result of air pollution and hurts plants and animals that live in water.

The largest rainfall that I measured with my rain gauge was _____ millimetres. That was quite a rain!

In the winter, you can measure snowfall with a ruler. Pick a flat spot that was shovelled or ploughed after the last snow fall and stick the ruler down through the snow to the ground. Because snow isn't always quite level, it's a good idea to take several measurements. Then find the average reading by adding together all your measurements and dividing by the number of measurements you made.

The largest snowfall at home while I was a Cub was _____ centimetres. (Write in your record with a pencil in case there is a larger snowfall later.)

When you've finished making your record of rainfall or snowfall, show it to your leaders and compare it with records made by other members of your six or pack.

A Bird Feeder

When you promised to do a good turn every day, did you ever think that you could do a good turn to birds as well as to people? During the winter, snow and ice bury most of the natural food supply of birds. You can help birds survive by keeping a bird feeder going all winter.

If you want to attract a lot of birds, start feeding them in the autumn before the snow falls. One thing is VERY IMPORTANT. If you start feeding birds in the fall, you must continue until spring. The birds will become dependent on your feeder. If you stop feeding them before they can find food somewhere else, many of them may die.

You can make a bird feeder in many different ways. Here are some of them:

1. Put half a coconut shell in a tree.
2. Cut a hole in the side of a milk carton and hang the carton in a tree.
3. Put a tray with sides on it almost anywhere.
4. Buy a feeder from a store. Maybe you can buy a kit and build it yourself.

Keep your feeder filled with wild bird seed. You can buy it in a grocery store or pet shop. You can also use bread crumbs, sunflower seeds, crushed corn, or unsalted nuts (too much salt is harmful to birds). Do not use peanut butter alone, as it might choke the bird. Be sure to mix seeds with any peanut butter you use.

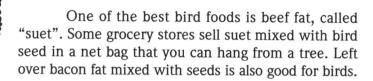

One of the best bird foods is beef fat, called "suet". Some grocery stores sell suet mixed with bird seed in a net bag that you can hang from a tree. Left over bacon fat mixed with seeds is also good for birds.

If you like, you can keep a record of all the different kinds of birds that use your feeder. Borrow a book from the library to help you identify them. You can use this information for your star requirement or your badge.

In the spring, tell your six, Akela, or one of your other leaders about your bird feeder. If you've kept a record of the different birds that use it, show them the record, too.

You can also make a bird bath or bird house. Bird baths are easy. Take an old garbage can lid and mount it on a tree stump or place it on the ground and surround it with a few rocks. Make sure you keep it filled with water.

Birds are fussy about where they build their nests. If you want to build a bird house, borrow a book about bird houses from the library and follow its directions. Make sure that the house you choose to build is a kind that a bird living in your area likes!

I saw these kinds of birds using my feeder or bird house:

_____

_____

_____

_____

Looking after the World

The more you use your eyes and ears to explore the world around you, the more you'll come to love it. And the more you love the world, the more you'll want to protect it. We hear a lot about pollution and damage to our environment these days. What can just one Wolf Cub do to protect the world against damage?

Plenty!

The first thing you can do is leave nature alone and let it look after itself. Everything in the natural world has its own place. If we go out and cut branches off living trees or catch frogs or snakes and carry them around to show our friends, or poke our fingers at birds' eggs, we disturb their place in nature and harm them. Let's use our eyes and ears to observe nature but let's not use our fingers too much!

The second thing you can do is clean up after yourself. Before you go home after an outing or a camp, you can help pick up every little scrap of litter you and the other Cubs dropped. Garbage can foul up water, make places look bad, and even become eaten by animals which mistake it for food. When you leave, try to make the place as clean as it was when you arrived — or even cleaner. Use garbage cans when you find them. If you can't find them, carry out the trash you carried in.

Things I can do to protect my natural world:

There are lots of other things you can do to protect your natural world. Maybe you can think up some of them yourself. Why don't you make a list of things you think up and share it with your six?

These are some of the things our six did to protect our natural world:

_____

_____

_____

You can also protect the environment when you are out camping. Write down some things you can do:

_____

_____

_____

_____

In my natural world, the two things
I did that I liked best were:

1. _____

_____

_____

2. _____

_____

_____

Some special things I learned were:

_____

_____

_____

_____

Some things I'd try next time:

_____

_____

_____

_____

4

CHAPTER 5

The Outdoors

Activity Area

hen B.-P. was young, he loved to get outdoors away from home and school to do things on his own. He built simple gadgets to help make camping easier. He learned to know where he was all the time, so he wouldn't get lost. He set up shelters to protect himself from the weather.

In fact, B.-P. was learning Wolf Cub outdoor skills, even though he didn't invent Wolf Cubs until many years later!

Outdoor skills are the things you can do to help keep yourself safe and comfortable when you're alone or with a few friends away from home.

Learning and practising outdoor skills with your leaders and the other Cubs can lead you to all kinds of adventures and fun. You can learn and do many of these outdoor skills with your parents and family, too.

In this chapter, you will learn some outdoor skills, and your leaders will help you learn others. Then, you will see how to use your outdoor skills to go exploring with your pack. When you go up to Scouts, you'll learn even more about outdoor skills.

Green Star Activities

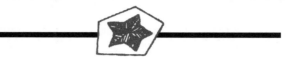

Green Star Activities will help you get started in learning the basic outdoor skills. If you're interested in how to camp and take care of yourself in the outdoors, try starting with these activities.

To earn the Green Star, choose and do any five of the A requirements and any three of the B requirements. These activities can be done by yourself, or with your six, pack, family or friends.

A Requirements

CHECK OFF WHEN COMPLETED AND WRITE THE DATE.

_____ ☐ 1. Estimate three distances and measure three things by using your body, such as the length of your foot, your pace or the top of your thumb.

1/25/12 ☑ 2. Tie and show a practical use for any five knots such as reef, sheet bend, taut-line, bowline, fisherman's knot, round turn and two half hitches, clove hitch.

_____ ☐ 3. Make a Cub First Aid/Survival kit.

_____ ☐ 4. Make or assemble a camp gadget for outdoor use.

11/16/11 ☑ 5. Know what to do if lost.

11/20/11 ☑ 6. Recognize or describe the signs for different types of weather.

11/19/11 ☑ 7. Lay, light and safely put out a fire in the outdoors.

1/16/11 ☑ 8. Show how to use a road or topographical map.

11/20/11 ☑ 9. Tell or demonstrate how to dress for different weather conditions to reduce the risk of hypothermia and reduce your exposure to the sun's ultraviolet rays.

11/6/11 ☑ 10. Know and explain some rules for protecting nature while on an outing.

B Requirements

CHECK OFF WHEN COMPLETED AND WRITE THE DATE.

11/20/11	☑	1. Take part in three pack hikes.
	☐	2. Help prepare and cook a hot meal on a family, six or pack outing.
11/16/11	☐	3. Tell or show how the sun, moon and North star can help you find directions.
11/16/11	☐	4. Make or follow a trail of not more than 300 metres using clues, trail signs, a map, compass directions or any combination of these.
	☐	5. Draw a simple sketch map of a campsite or your Cub meeting place using compass and paces.
	☐	6. Without harming nature, put up and take down an emergency shelter of your own design.

I completed my Green Star requirements on:

3/18/12   CB Paynter
(date)

Badge Activities

If you enjoy learning outdoor skills, and want to learn more, here are some challenging activities you might like to try. These activities can be done by yourself, or with your six, pack, family or friends.

Camping Badge

CHECK OFF WHEN COMPLETED AND WRITE THE DATE.

_2010_ ☑ 1. Do one of the following:
  a) Complete 4 days of family camping (they don't need to be all together).
  b) Take part in two Cub camps.

_____ ☐ 2. Make a list of some safety and hygiene rules for camping and discuss these with your leader.

_____ ☐ 3. Make a list of personal camping gear needed for sleeping, eating, clothing and first aid at an overnight camp. Discuss this list with your leader.

_____ ☐ 4. Describe what to do if lost.

_____ ☐ 5. In any season, do any 5 of the following:

☑ a) Put up and take down a simple outdoor shelter or tent.

☑ b) Cook a simple meal over an open fire or portable stove.

☐ c) Show how to use a compass.

☑ d) Help in doing two different camp chores or duties.

☐ e) Show how to properly dispose of camp garbage or waste while camping.

☐ f) Show how to purify drinking water at camp.

☐ g) Using appropriate knots, erect a pole or line on which to hang your gear.

☐ h) Show how to keep food safe from insects and animals.

☐ i) Show how to safely handle a pocket knife or camp saw.

_____ ☐ 6. Be aware of and explain no-trace camping.

I completed my Camping Badge requirements on:

_____
 (date)

Cooking Badge

CHECK OFF WHEN COMPLETED AND WRITE THE DATE.

With the help of an adult, describe some safety rules for cooking on a stove, microwave, or around an open fire. Then, do any five of the following:

_____	☐ 1. Make some hot oatmeal.
Oct. 17	☑ 2. Cook a hotdog or hamburger.
_____	☐ 3. Use a tinfoil cup or orange half and bake a muffin in it.
_____	☐ 4. Wrap a potato in tinfoil and bake it in a fire.
Nov. 16	☑ 5. Boil water and cook some pasta of your choice.
Oct. 17	☑ 6. Make pancakes or french toast.
_____	☐ 7. Make biscuit or bannock dough and cook it on a stick or in a cup.
_____	☐ 8. Cook a baked apple, banana, or a tinfoil dessert of your choice.
Oct. 17	☑ 9. Make a campfire treat, such as SMOR's or popcorn.
_____	☐ 10. Cook a meal of your choice while at camp.
_____	☐ 11. Make a shish-ka-bob of meat and vegetables and cook over a fire.
Nov. 6	☑ 12. Cook an egg.

I completed my Cooking Badge requirements on:

Nov. 16 ＪＪＢ

(date)

Fishing Badge

CHECK OFF WHEN COMPLETED AND WRITE THE DATE.

_____ ☐ 1. Describe some safety rules for being in or around water, and know how to prevent and treat injuries caused by fish hooks and fish knives.

_____ ☐ 2. Show how to put together and use an angling outfit, a handline outfit, or an ice fishing outfit.

_____ ☐ 3. Name and identify some major sport fish in your area.

_____ ☐ 4. Describe the most suitable way to catch one sport fish of your choice.

_____ ☐ 5. Discuss the rules and regulations for fishing in your area, how to unhook and release a fish without harming it, and the benefits of using barbless hooks.

_____ ☐ 6. Do EITHER (a) or (b):

    a) Without help (except for the actual landing), catch three separate species of local fish. Name them correctly and describe what family they belong to and their place in fishing (game fish, minnow, coarse, etc.).

    b) Discuss water pollution in your area - how it can affect fishing and what can be done to reduce or eliminate pollution.

I completed my Fishing Badge requirements on:

_____
    (date)

Hiking Badge

CHECK OFF WHEN COMPLETED AND WRITE THE DATE.

_____ ☐ 1. Know how to take care of your feet for everyday walking, through washing, toenail clipping, wearing clean, dry socks and having proper fitting shoes.

_____ ☐ 2. Know how to treat a blister on the foot, insect bites, hypothermia, overheating and discuss the importance of getting adequate rest while hiking.

_____ ☐ 3. Discuss some safety rules for hiking, such as:
   a) staying with the group and using a buddy system
   b) keeping to designated trails
   c) keeping the group together
   d) having enough drinking water and food
   e) carrying a first aid kit, whistle and spare clothes.

_____ ☐ 4. Describe what to do if lost.

_____ ☐ 5. Know some rules for protecting nature when hiking.

_____ ☐ 6. Go on four hikes of one to two hours long, some of which could be in a conservation area or park, around your camp, around your community, or at night.

_____ ☐ 7. Prepare a nutritional trail mix to eat and share.

I completed my Hiking Badge requirements on:

_____

(date)

Trailcraft Badge

CHECK OFF WHEN COMPLETED AND WRITE THE DATE.

_____ ☐ 1. In preparing for a trip, know how to do the following:
   a) Tell an adult where you are going and include arrival time, route and any phone numbers.
   b) Wear clothes and shoes suitable for where you will be and the weather.
   c) Make a "footprint" by placing a sheet of tinfoil on a towel and then stepping on it with your shoes on. Mark the foil with your name and leave with an adult so searchers can identify your footprint if needed.
   d) Understand and use the buddy system when on trips.
   e) List some rules for preventing getting lost, such as staying on trails and with your group.

_____ ☐ 2. Discuss and demonstrate how to do the following if lost:
   a) Stay calm and slow down to save energy and body heat.
   b) Keep your head and body warm and dry to avoid hypothermia.
   c) Find a friendly place near a clearing and stay put to help searchers find you.
   d) Make a survival shelter or bed to keep off the cold ground and stay dry.
   e) Avoid eating strange berries and drinking unpurified water.
   f) Put out something bright for people to see.
   g) Make a pattern of three signals.
   h) Look big to airplanes by lying down in a clearing and wearing bright clothing or a coloured garbage bag.
   i) How to be careful around bodies of water.
   j) Yell back at any scary night noises.

_____ ☐ 3. Make a survival/first aid kit that includes among the items a high energy snack, several brightly coloured garbage bags, reflector or hand mirror and a whistle.

I completed my Trailcraft Badge requirements on:

_____

(date)

Watercraft Badge

CHECK OFF WHEN COMPLETED AND WRITE THE DATE.

Oct, 17 ☑ 1. Describe six different types of watercraft.

Oct. 17 ☑ 2. Correctly name and point out six different parts of a watercraft.

_____ ☐ 3. Explain and show the correct way to choose and wear a life jacket or Personal Flotation Device (PFD).

_____ ☐ 4. Demonstrate how to safely enter, change places in and exit a boat, showing how to move calmly and keep your weight low and centred. Know how to behave in a boat.

_____ ☐ 5. Describe the signs of dangerous weather and water conditions for boating, and what to do when you see them.

_____ ☐ 6. Demonstrate the following:
a) Identify three examples of good throwing assists.
b) Be able to throw a throwing assist (without a line) to a person at least two metres away.

_____ ☐ 7. Demonstrate the following:
a) While wearing your PFD, curl up in a ball to form the Heat Escape Lessening Position (HELP) to keep warm in the water.
b) With a small group who are all wearing PFD's, huddle together to make the HUDDLE position to keep you and others warm in the water.

_____ ☐ 8. Know the importance of staying with your boat if you fall out or tip over.

_____ ☐ 9. With a buddy or adult, launch a boat and row, paddle or sail in a straight line for 50 metres; turn and come back.

I completed my Watercraft Badge requirements on:

_____
(date)

Winter Cubbing Badge

CHECK OFF WHEN COMPLETED AND WRITE THE DATE.

_____ ☐ 1. Describe how to prevent and treat:
a) Frost-bite
b) Skin on cold metal
c) Snow blindness
d) Breaking through ice
e) Hypothermia

_____ ☐ 2. Show that you are properly dressed for a winter outing or describe how to dress for winter weather. Know the importance of staying dry.

_____ ☐ 3. Recognize and identify in winter conditions three common birds and three common trees or shrubs.

_____ ☐ 4. Point out the North Star and *three* night sky features, such as stars, constellations, and planets.

20/0/14 ☑ 5. Take part in two of the following:
2012
ⓐ a winter camp
b) a winter hike
c) two winter outdoor meetings
d) lighting a fire and cooking a simple meal under winter conditions
ⓔ a hike on snowshoes or skis
f) an ice fishing trip

I completed my Winter Cubbing Badge requirements on:

_____

(date)

The Outdoor Awards

If you are really keen on outdoor activities and want to expand your knowledge, try this award, or the next award. They require a lot of skill, but you'll be a great camper when you are done! These activities can be done by yourself, or with your six, pack, family or friends.

Canadian Camper Award

CHECK OFF WHEN COMPLETED AND WRITE THE DATE.

To achieve this award, you must complete the following:

Feb. 2011   ☐ 1. Earn the Green Star.
   ☑ 2. Earn the First Aider Badge.
   ☐ 3. Earn the Camping Badge.
2011   ☑ 4. Participate in at least three Cub camps.
   ☐ 5. With a buddy and help from your leader, choose a campsite and complete the following:
     a) Set up a shelter of your own design or a tent. Weather permitting, spend a whole night sleeping in your shelter.
     b) Where permitted, build a fire and boil a cup of water.
     c) Scout the area and discover what you can about the terrain, kinds of plants and habits of local wildlife.
     d) Locate the direction of North and predict possible changes in weather.
   ☐ 6. Help show other Cubs how to do a camping skill of your choice.
   ☐ 7. Where possible, visit a Scout troop camp and learn about their camping program.

I completed my Canadian Camper Award requirements on:

_____

(date)

This Award may be worn on your Scout sash after you become a Scout.

84

Canadian Heritage Trails Award

CHECK OFF WHEN COMPLETED AND WRITE THE DATE.

To achieve this award, you must complete the following:

_____ ☐ 1. Earn the Green Star.
_____ ☑ 2. Earn the Hiking or Watercraft Badge.
_____ ☐ 3. Locate a trail or waterway and learn
                         about its heritage importance.
_____ ☐ 4. Travel on this route, and list some of the signifi-
                         cant natural or heritage features along the way.
_____ ☐ 5. While travelling on this route, participate in
                         a project that helps restore, clean or
                         preserve the section you are on.

I completed my Canadian Heritage Trails Award requirements on:

_____

(date)

This Award may be worn on your Scout sash after you become a Scout.

A Cub First Aid/ Survival Kit

Think of some things that might happen to you when you're out on your own.

For example:
A friend scrapes his knee.
You cut your finger.
You are lost and cold and want to build a fire.

What could you carry with you to help you deal with these problems? A First Aid/Survival kit provides some basic equipment to help you in an emergency.

Start with a container to keep your articles in. It needs to be small enough so that you can carry it in your backpack wherever you go. The best kit in the world is no good to you if it's back home in your cupboard when you need to use it.

It also needs to be strong and waterproof. The best container will probably be made out of tough plastic. If you can't find one at home, try the local hardware or discount store.

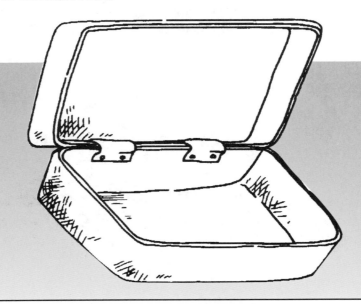

When you have your container, tape your name, address, and telephone number on the inside, and then think about what you should carry in it. Here are some suggestions:

First Aid Kit Part

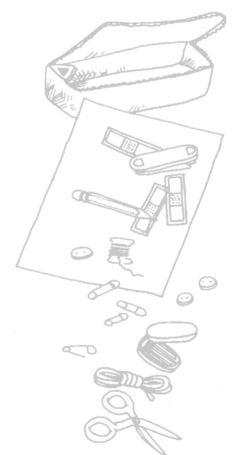

☐ 1. Adhesive bandages, assorted sizes

☐ 2. Gauze pads

☐ 3. Adhesive tape

☐ 4. Safety pins

☐ 5. Tweezers

☐ 6. Coins (for emergency phone calls)

☐ 7. Paper and pencil (for writing down emergency information)

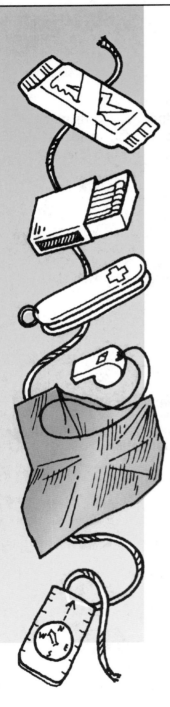

Survival Kit Part

☐ 1. High energy snack (granola bar, dried fruit and peanuts)
☐ 2. Waterproofed matches
☐ 3. Small pocket knife
☐ 4. Brightly coloured large plastic garbage bags (for shelter and signalling)
☐ 5. Whistle and mirror
☐ 6. Nylon or strong string
☐ 7. Aluminum foil (to make cooking and drinking utensils)
☐ 8. Compass

When you've made your Cub First Aid/Survival Kit, show it to one of your leaders, your sixer and your six.

I made my First Aid/Survival Kit on:

_____

I put it into this type of container:

_____

I keep my kit in my:

_____

In it, I carry all the things I've checked off on the list above.

Avoiding Sunburns

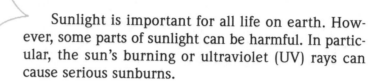

Sunlight is important for all life on earth. However, some parts of sunlight can be harmful. In particular, the sun's burning or ultraviolet (UV) rays can cause serious sunburns.

The earth's ozone layer - a thin layer of gas high above the earth - acts to block out UV rays. In the past few years, the ozone layer has become slightly thinner due to air pollution. This means that more of the sun's UV rays can now reach the ground and us.

There are ways to protect you and your family from getting too much UV rays and a bad sunburn. Here are some tips.

- Use a sunscreen lotion that has a SPF number of 15 or higher. SPF stands for "Sun Protection Factor" and refers to the lotion's ability to stop your skin from burning. The higher the SPF number, the longer you can stay in the sun. If it takes 10 minutes to burn your skin, an SPF 15 sunscreen will give you 150 minutes of protection.
- Use sunscreen often if you are swimming, and don't forget to put it on your nose, ears, tops of your feet and the backs of your knees.
- Use protective clothing, such as lightweight cotton pants and long sleeved shirts.
- Use a wide brimmed hat to protect your head and shield your eyes.
- Use sunglasses that screen out UV light.
- Avoid being in too much sun from 10 am - 3 pm., when UV rays are the strongest.

Lost Prevention Tips

Hiking and camping are great activities for adventure. But before going off on a trip, you need to know how to prevent becoming lost, and what to do if you happen to get separated from friends and family. Here are a few tips.

Before Going on a Trip

- Tell your family where you are going, when you will arrive, the route you plan on taking, and any local phone numbers.
- Dress for the weather and pack a few extra clothes in case it gets cold or wet.
- Use the "buddy system" which means going with a friend and never alone.
- Stay on trails and with your group. Don't take unknown shortcuts.
- Always pack along your First Aid/Survival kit.

If You Do Get Lost

- Stay calm and relax. Someone will come to find you. Don't climb up a tree or hide under logs.
- Keep warm. Cover your head and zip up your jacket.
- Find a sheltered place near a clearing and stay put to help searchers find you. Don't wander around.
- If night comes, make a survival shelter or bed to keep you off the cold ground and to help you stay dry. Make a small fire if it is cold out.
- Put out something bright. One of your coloured garbage bags can be ripped into strips.
- If it is cold and wet, rip a hole in a garbage bag for your head and put it on as a raincoat.
- Make three signals - fires, whistles or yells - to alert searchers where you are.
- Don't worry about being punished. Adults are only concerned about finding you safe and healthy.

5

Lighting Fires Safely

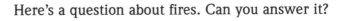

Every Cub wants to learn to light a fire that will stay lit. In Cubs, you have a chance to learn how to make a fire that will light almost every time — even in the rain, if you're careful.

Here's a question about fires. Can you answer it?

Q. What's the first thing you have to think about when you want to lay and light a fire?

A. The first thing to think about is how you're going to put the fire out.

Did you guess the right answer? Think about it for a minute. What do you think would happen if you lit a fire and couldn't put it out? It could be very dangerous for you and everyone and everything near you.

Here are the most important safety rules about fires:

1. Before you light it, make sure you can put it out. Keep lots of water or sand nearby to put your fire out.

2. Never light a fire unless one of your leaders or a parent is with you, except in an emergency.

3. Build a fire in an approved fire circle or park grill. If this is not available, dig a pit in the open and away from grass, leaves, and roots. Try to keep the fire small. Save the sod and soil, and use it to cover up the pit once your fire is out cold.

4. Check the wind direction and make sure that sparks won't blow away and cause a fire nearby.
5. Never leave a fire unattended. Gather all the wood you need before starting a fire. Watch it carefully until you put it out.
6. Never play with a fire or near a fire.
7. Be sure the fire is completely out before you leave it. Pour water on it, stir the ashes, and pour on more water. Be sure you tidy up before you leave.

If you follow these safety rules, you can be sure your fire won't get out of control.

To make your fire burn properly, you need three things: tinder to get it started; kindling to keep it going; and fuel to provide heat.

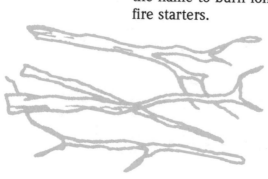

Tinder is thin, dry stuff that lights easily and burns quickly. You can use paper for tinder, but it's better to practise using other things so that you can light a fire even if you don't have paper. Some other things that make good tinder are birch-bark you find on the ground, dry brown grass, dry twigs at the base of fir or pine trees, and dead leaves. Whatever you do, NEVER peel the bark from live trees. The bark is their skin and, if you peel it off, you will likely kill them. You can also make tinder by cutting a milk carton into strips. The wax coating will cause the flame to burn longer. These strips are also called fire starters.

Kindling is twigs and small sticks that will catch fire from the tinder and burn long enough to light the fuel. Make sure your kindling is dead and dry: not every stick that looks dead is dead. If the weather is wet, you can find dry kindling by breaking dead sticks off trees, but be sure they are dead first. If you're not sure, ask one of your leaders to show you.

For fuel, you need bigger sticks about the size of a broom handle. These sticks are harder to light - which is why you need tinder and kindling to get the fire started - but once they catch fire, they will burn for a long time and give lots of heat.

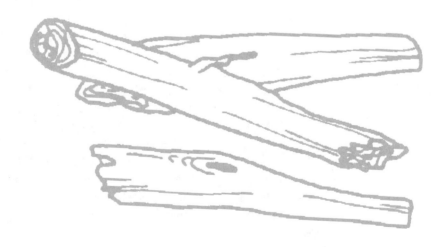

Fire Making

The tepee fire, which looks like a native tepee, is an easy fire to make. Here's how to do it.

1. Before you start, make sure you have enough fuel to keep your fire going and you can put the fire out when finished.
2. Place a fire starter and a large handful of tinder on the ground. You can use strips of a milk carton as a fire starter.
3. Push a stick into the ground and slant it over the tinder.
4. Make a tepee of kindling sticks by leaning them across the stick you pushed into the ground. Towards the wind, leave an opening - like a door - to your tepee.
5. Crouch down in front of the opening with your back to the wind.
6. Strike a match (wooden matches are best), let it burn into a real flame, and carefully touch it to the tinder, close to the ground.
7. Let the kindling in the tepee get a good start, then slowly feed the fire with thin pieces of fuel. If you add fuel too quickly, you may put out the fire.
8. Slowly add fuel wood until the fire is the size you want.
9. If the flame begins to die out or smoke, your fire may not be getting enough air. Gently blow or fan the flame until the fire gets going again.

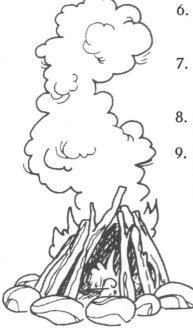

A tepee fire is great for boiling water or heating baked beans or other foods in your cooking pot. If you want to cook other things such as baked potatoes or baked apples, you need a kind of fire that burns down into hot coals. Ask a sixer or one of your leaders to help you make one.

I lit my first fire on an outing to _____.

I needed _____ *matches. This is what I used for*

tinder _____

kindling _____

_____

bigger fuel _____.

_____

I used my fire to _____

and it was (circle ONE)

    a fizzle

    OK

    neat

    awesome!

Outdoor Cooking

Nothing tastes better than food you cook yourself, especially when you're outdoors. Ask one of your leaders or your sixer if the pack or your six can go on a cook out so that you can try your hand at being a great chef!

The easiest way to cook outdoors is to heat up some tinned food in your cooking pot over a teepee fire. Do you like baked beans? Stew? Just empty the can into your cooking pot and hang it over the fire until it's hot. Keep stirring the food or you may find that it is burned on the bottom and cold on top. Wear a pair of old gloves or use pot pliers to remove the pot so you don't burn yourself.

If you like wieners and beans, you can cut up a wiener and stir it into the pot with the beans. Or you can stick it onto the end of a strong green stick (one that isn't dead and dry) and hold it over the fire. You know the wiener is done when the skin starts popping and crackling.

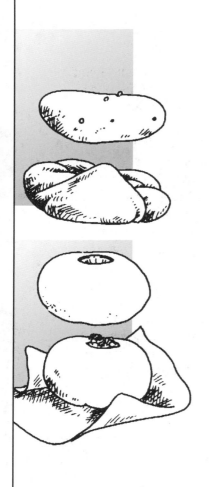

How about a baked potato or baked apple? Get these foods ready at home before you go on the cook out. Here's what you do.

Baked Potato

1. Wash the potato thoroughly. Leave on the skin. Poke holes in the skin to let any steam out.
2. Wrap the potato in a layer of heavy duty aluminum foil with the dull side out. Fold together the edges carefully so that there are no gaps or bulges.
3. Wrap the potato in a second layer of heavy duty aluminum foil as carefully as you did with the first layer.

Baked Apple

1. Take the core out of the apple with a kitchen corer.
2. Fill the hole with something sweet. Try raisins, marshmallows, cinnamon, a bit of sugar, even some pieces of chocolate.
3. Wrap the apple in two layers of aluminum foil in the same way you did the potato.

When you pack the potato and apple to take on your cook out, protect them so that you don't put a hole in the aluminum foil.

To bake a potato or an apple, you need a fire with good hot coals. Ask Akela to show you how to make one and be patient. It takes a while for the coals to get hot.

When the coals are ready, carefully put the potato in the middle of them and let it bake for one hour.

When the potato is half done, put your apple in the coals. It takes half an hour to bake and, if you time it right, your apple and potato will be ready at the same time. Pull your packages out of the fire with a stick and let them sit for a minute while the aluminum foil cools a bit. Then, if you open it carefully, you can use the foil for your dish. Add butter or margarine and salt and pepper to your potato if you like, and you have a meal fit for royalty - or even a Cub! Remember to dispose of the used foil or other garbage properly. If animals eat garbage it can make them sick. Garbage also attracts animals to campsites, where they can bother or hurt those campers who use the campsite next.

If you really want to try something challenging and fun, ask one of your leaders to help you cook a foil dinner.

This was my first fire cook out menu: _____

_____

_____

_____

It tasted (circle ONE):

YUCK   HMM

OK   YUMM

FANTASTIC !!

Knots

Knots are a fun part of Cubbing. When you learn to tie knots, you learn to make loops that won't slip, tie together two different kinds of rope, tie on a bandage properly, shorten a rope on a tent, and lash a rope to a pole. The great thing about knots is that they are fun to learn, fun to practise using, and really handy when you have to use rope in a hurry. So, let's have some fun! Remember to collect all rope or string after using it, and take apart all rope projects done in the woods before going home.

Reef Knot

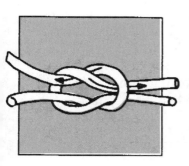

This is also called a square knot and it's probably one of the most common knots to use. You use a reef knot to tie together two ropes of the same size or to tie on a bandage or an arm sling properly. The little verse that goes with it describes what you do with the two ends of rope as you tie it. It says "left over right and right over left". What did you use your reef knot for?

_____

_____

Sheet Bend

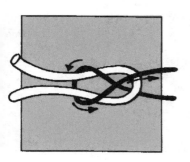

Did you ever try to tie together two different kinds of rope? Notice how the thin rope jams against the loop of the thick one. The sheet bend is a good knot for tying together two different sizes of rope, but you can also use it to tie together two ropes of equal size. What did you use a sheet bend for?

_____

_____

Bowline

This makes a loop that won't slip, no matter how hard you pull on it. You can use it to make a leash for your dog or a hand hold on a rope you're using to pull something. You can even slip it under the arms of an unconscious person so that you can hoist the person to safety. What did you use a bowline for?

_____

_____

Round Turn and Two Half Hitches

This is an easy way to tie a rope to a pole, ring or bucket handle. It's great for towing things. What did you use a round turn and two half hitches for?

_____

_____

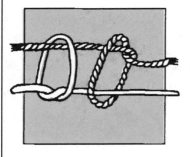

Clove Hitch

This is another way to tie a rope to a pipe, tree, or pole. It's a good knot to use for clotheslines and, in Scouts, you'll use it a lot for pioneer work. What did you use a clove hitch for?

_____

_____

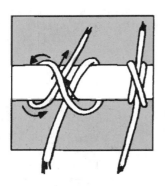

Fisherman's Knot

This knot helps you tie together two pieces of line — some twine and fishing line, for example. What did you use a fisherman's knot for?

_____

_____

Tautline Hitch

The tautline hitch is an adjustable hitch, allowing you to tighten or loosen the rope. It is used for tying tent or tarp guide lines.

Clothing and Equipment for the Outdoors

Explorers always make sure that they have the proper clothing and equipment. You'll want to have the right equipment for the exploring you do, too. The clothes you wear and the equipment you take will depend on where you are planning to go. Think very carefully about what you will need and listen to Akela's advice.

5

CAMPING CHECKLIST

(Will vary according to season and weather)

WEAR *(or carry in top of pack)*
- ☐ Camp clothes/uniform
- ☐ Hiking shoes
- ☐ Sweater or jacket
- ☐ Raincoat or poncho
- ☐ Rubbers, lightweight
- ☐ Toque, ball cap, or wide brimmed hat
- ☐ Watch

CARRY IN POCKETS
- ☐ Handkerchief/tissues
- ☐ Wallet and money (include a quarter for a phone call)
- ☐ Compass
- ☐ Sunscreen
- ☐ Sunglasses

TOP OR OUTSIDE POCKETS OF PACK
- ☐ First Aid/Survival kit
- ☐ Repair kit: rubber bands, shoe laces, wire strand, paper clips
- ☐ Sewing kit: needle, thread
- ☐ Personal toilet paper in plastic bag
- ☐ Extra plastic bags
- ☐ Pair of extra socks
- ☐ Eating utensils: knife, fork, spoon, cup, deep sided plate, bowl
- ☐ Flashlight, extra batteries
- ☐ Map
- ☐ Canteen

INSIDE PACK OR SECURED TO PACK OR FRAME
- ☐ Sleeping bag or two or three warm blankets (if outside pack, covered completely with water-proof plastic)

INSIDE PACK

☐ *Waterproof ground cloth, plastic*
☐ *Sneakers*
☐ *Plastic or cloth clothesbag containing: extra shirt, extra pants, pyjamas or sweat suit, extra handkerchief, extra socks, change of underwear*
☐ *Toilet kit containing: washcloth, comb, soap in waterproof container, hand towel, bath towel, metal mirror, toothbrush and paste/powder*

OPTIONAL ITEMS

☐ *Songbook*
☐ *Camera, film*
☐ *Notebook, pencil*
☐ *Binoculars*
☐ *Nature books*
☐ *Cub handbook*
☐ *Insect repellant*
☐ *Swim trunks*
☐ *Rope or line*
☐ *Air mattress or foam pad*
☐ *Washbasin, plastic or canvas*
☐ *Air pillow*
☐ *Personal tent*
☐ *Bible, Testament, or Prayer Book, according to faith*
☐ *Campfire blanket*

Tip: To prevent your flashlight from turning on in your pack, put the batteries in backwards until you need to use it.

Here are some suggestions for clothing and equipment you should have for different kinds of outings.

Winter Outings

1. Boots with removable felt liners. Never wear rubber boots in winter. Make sure your snow boots aren't too tight.
2. Two pairs of wool socks, if they don't make your boots fit too tightly.
3. Insulated nylon snowpants
4. Wool pants and thermal long underwear
5. Insulated nylon jacket with hood
6. Long sleeve shirt and sweater. It's good to have several thin layers instead of one thick layer. If you get too hot, you can cool down by taking off a layer. It's important not to get too hot and sweaty in winter because, if you do, your clothes will get wet, and you will get cold.
7. Hat that covers your ears. In cold weather, most heat is lost from your head. Keep it covered, even at night while you sleep.
8. Face mask, neck warmer, or scarf to protect your face.
9. Mitts. They are warmer than gloves. Wear two pairs, if possible.

10. First Aid/Survival kit in your jacket pocket.
11. Small kit bag to carry the things below.
12. Extra socks
13. Extra mitts
14. High-energy snacks. Nuts, raisins, granola, and chocolate are foods that can give you energy in a hurry.
15. Strong plastic bags. They are useful for many things. If your boots leak, put the bags on your feet inside the boots. Be sure your socks are dry. You can also put dry clothes or things you collect along the way in plastic bags.
16. Ground sheet or strong plastic sheet to make an emergency shelter to protect you from the wind.
17. Waterproof matches
18. A candle for a quick source of heat
19. Sunglasses to prevent snow blindness.

Remember: Wind makes the temperature much colder and takes away body heat. On windy days, put on extra clothes, watch out for frostbite, and stay in sunny, sheltered areas.

Summer Outings

You don't need as much equipment to protect you in the summer, but here are some things you should bring.

1. First Aid/Survival kit
2. Hat to protect you against sunstroke. A hat with a wide brim all around gives the best protection to eyes, ears and the back of your neck. A ball cap is next best.
3. Insect repellent
4. Sun screen with high SPF (Sun Protection Factor)
5. Rain poncho
6. Sturdy footwear like good running shoes or walking or hiking boots
7. Sunglasses to protect your eyes.
8. Extra socks. Sweaty socks can cause blisters.
9. Lightweight long sleeved shirt and pants for sun protection.
10. Water

Spring and Autumn Outings

In late autumn and early spring, the weather can turn cold very quickly. Bring the same clothing and equipment you would for a winter expedition.

Remember, to be an explorer, you need to keep working on these three things.

1. Keep your eyes open and know where you are.
2. Know and practise your Wolf Cub skills.
3. Carry the proper clothing and equipment for each expedition.

Now for some exploring!

Camping

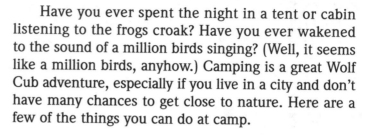

Have you ever spent the night in a tent or cabin listening to the frogs croak? Have you ever wakened to the sound of a million birds singing? (Well, it seems like a million birds, anyhow.) Camping is a great Wolf Cub adventure, especially if you live in a city and don't have many chances to get close to nature. Here are a few of the things you can do at camp.

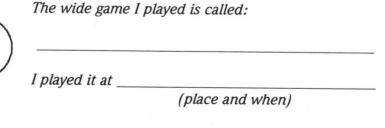

1. Practise your outdoor skills. Ask a sixer or one of your leaders to show you how to put up a tent. Learn how to work as a team to set up your camp. Practise living comfortably in the small space of a tent.

This is one thing I learned in setting up a camp site:

_____

2. Play wide games. Instead of the Cub hall, you can use the whole of your camp area for games.

The wide game I played is called:

_____

I played it at _____
                  (place and when)

This is how to play it:

_____

_____

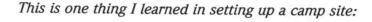

3. Try stalking - walking through the woods without making a sound. You have to watch every step you make. Can you creep up on your leaders without them hearing you? It's not easy but it's fun.

4. Look at the stars. Away from the smog and lights of the city, the stars are amazingly bright. If you watch carefully, you may even see an orbiting satellite.

These are the constellations, planets or other things I saw:

_____

_____

5. Listen to the sounds of nature: frogs, birds, wind in the long grass, rain on the tent roof. We think of nature as being peaceful, but sometimes it's very noisy!

The sounds I heard were:

_____

_____

I heard a mystery sound and I think what made it looked like this:

Hiking

If you go on a day hike, you can do some of the things you do at camp. Here are a few other things you can try, too.

1. Go on a winter hike. Practise cross country skiing or walking on snowshoes. Learn to find dry firewood in the snow. Pretend that you're caught in a storm and set up a shelter to protect you from the weather.

This is what my shelter looked like:

2. Explore a particular trail. Maybe one of your leaders can mark a route using trail signs and you can try to find the correct path.

This is what I saw on the trail:

_____

_____

_____

3. Go on a blindfold walk. Led by a leader, a few Cubs wear blindfolds and hold on to a rope. As you walk, try to sense everything without using your eyes. Are you in the sun or the shade? Is the ground rough or smooth? Which way is the wind blowing? Are you in trees or in the open? What do you smell? Hear?

This is what I remember from my blindfold walk:

_____

_____

4. Pretend you are a small animal and try to see the world as it does. Lie on your stomach and look through the grass. What do you see? Try it at noon. Try it in the early morning or evening when the sun is low.

5. Be a raccoon. Hold in your thumb and walk on all fours, feeling things with just your fingers. Try to identify the things you feel without using your eyes.

Being a raccoon was:

_____

_____

6. Point out landmarks while hiking. These will help you remember where you are. Look behind you when hiking so you will remember what the trail looks like when coming back.

The landmarks I saw while on a hike were:

_____

_____

_____

_____

_____

_____

_____

_____

5

GORDTOWN

YONGE STREET

Outdoor Gadgets

A gadget is something simple you can put together to help make things easier for you in the outdoors, at home or wherever you are. There are hundreds of outdoor gadgets you can make if you want to. Another Cub, one of your leaders, or your parents can probably suggest a few that might be fun to try. Start with this list and add some ideas of your own.

- water can rack
- uniform hanger
- pack rack
- book marker
- snow goggles
- camp chair
- sewing kit
- pot holder
- fire starter kit
- home made cup
- a whistle

Cooking Pot Gadget

Here is a gadget you can make to use on a cookout or at camp. You start with a tin can and you end up with a cooking pot!

You need:

5

1. A large tin can
   - 1.36 L (48 fl. oz.).
   A juice can is good.

2. Strong wire - 40-50 cm long

3. A hammer and a
   7.5 cm long nail

4. A piece of wood about as
   long as the can is wide

5. A can opener

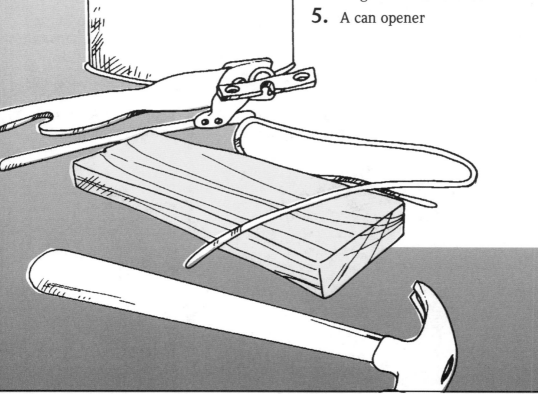

How to make it:

1. Take the lid off the can and make sure there are no sharp edges.

2. Wash the can in hot water and soap.

3. Wedge the piece of wood into the top of the can. You may have to bend the can a bit so that it fits fairly tightly.

4. Hammer the nail through the can a little way into the piece of wood (you might have to ask someone to hold the can for you while you are hammering). This is to make a hole in the can. Pull out the nail, then hammer it a little way into the other end of the wood, on the exact opposite side of the can. Pull out the nail again.

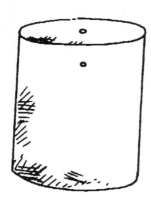

5. Remove the piece of wood. Smooth out the sharp edges of the holes in the can. You may be able to bang them flat with the hammer or you can remove them with a metal file.

6. String the wire through the holes in the can to make a handle. Twist the ends of the wire around the handle to hold it on firmly.

7. When you go on your cook out, fill your cooking pot with baked beans, stew, or water for instant soup mix, and hang it over your fire. Stir it now and again so that your supper doesn't burn!

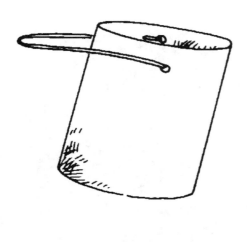

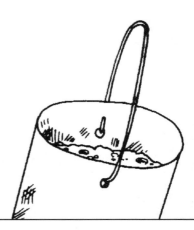

This is what my gadget looked like.

Compass

A compass is a valuable camping tool. Knowing what direction you are going is important when taking trips.

If you look at a compass, you will see a needle with a red tip. The needle is magnetic and always points north. Around the needle is the compass housing. On it are numbers from 1 - 360. These are called degrees. They are used to tell what direction, or bearing, you are going.

How to Use a Compass

Let's say you want to go west. Turn the compass housing until 270 degrees is lined up with the direction arrow on the outside of the compass base. Now slowly turn your body until the compass needle is within the large orienteering arrow found inside the housing. Remember to keep the compass flat, and away from your belt buckle or other metal that attracts magnets.

Now that you are facing west, look ahead and pick out a land mark, such as a tall tree or a rock, that is in line with the direction arrow. As long as you walk towards that landmark, you will be heading west.

Make a Map

Here's how to make a map of your campsite. Stand in the centre of camp with your compass and find north. Take a piece of paper and write north at the top. Point your direction arrow at various spots in your camp. Record what degree they are at and how many steps, or paces they are away from where you are standing.

For making the map, make 1 cm equal to 1 pace. Place the compass on the middle of the paper. Set the compass to point north (360 degrees) and line up the paper so the top also points north. Pretend your tent is at 20 degrees and 5 paces away. Find 20 degrees on the compass and mark it on the paper. Now draw a line from the paper's centre through the 20 degree mark so it is 5 cm long. Draw a small tent to show this is where your tent is. When you are done doing this for everything in camp, you will have an accurate camp map.

5

Trail Signs

Trail marking and trail reading are among the most useful and interesting Scouting skills you will learn. Start with simple trail signs when hiking and playing games, then go on to reading and following the tracks of birds, animals, and human beings, and interpreting the stories they tell.

Trail signs can be made with chalk, stones, twigs or grass, as shown in the sketches below.

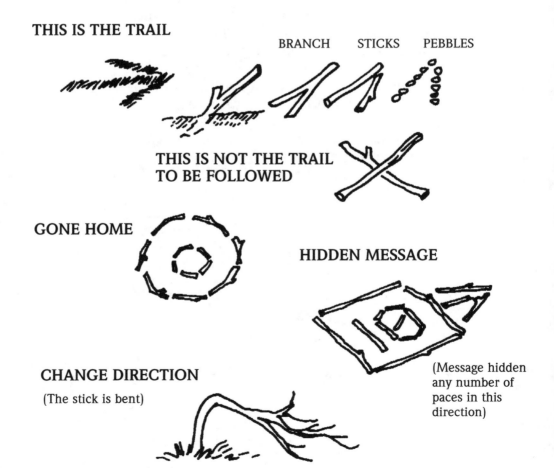

THIS IS THE TRAIL

BRANCH   STICKS   PEBBLES

**THIS IS NOT THE TRAIL
TO BE FOLLOWED**

GONE HOME

HIDDEN MESSAGE

CHANGE DIRECTION

(The stick is bent)

(Message hidden any number of paces in this direction)

The three outdoor skills I learned and used most were:

1._____

_____

2._____

_____

3._____

_____

Some special things I learned to do with these skills are:

_____

_____

_____

_____

_____

_____

_____

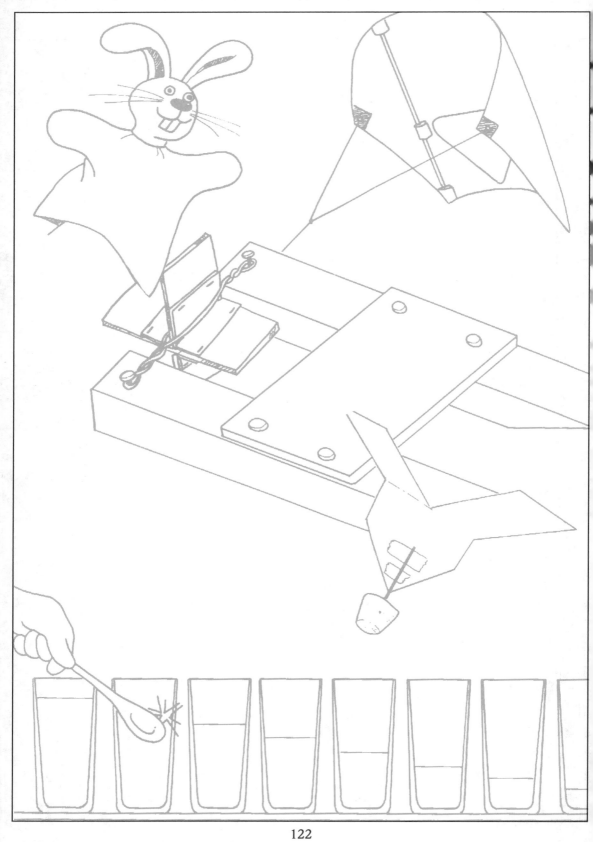

CHAPTER 6

Creative
Expression

Activity Area

o you like to create things? You can get a lot of satisfaction from working with your mind and hands to make something new, whether you are writing a story, building a model, or drawing a picture.

If you like to sing, dance, make models, paint, take pictures and use your imagination, here are some ideas for you to try. Lots of them are easy enough to do all by yourself. Others are a little bit harder, and you might want to ask your parents or an adult friend to help you. Or, maybe you could ask one of your leaders to help the whole pack make them.

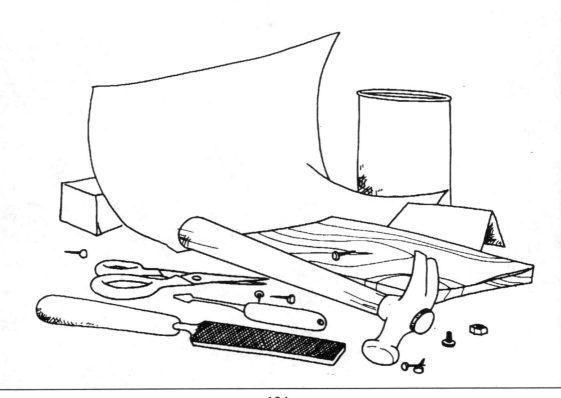

Tawny Star Activities

The Tawny Star Activities will give you a whole variety of creative activities. Try as many as you like and let your imagination go wild! To earn the Tawny Star, choose and do any six of the A requirements and any three of the B requirements. These activities can be done by yourself, or with your six, pack, family or friends.

A Requirements

CHECK OFF WHEN COMPLETED AND WRITE THE DATE.

_____ ☐ 1. Show how to safely use simple tools, including a pocket knife.

_____ ☐ 2. Make a simple article such as a puppet, toy or game, papier-mâché item, woggle, etc.

__Oct. 14__ ☐ 3. Type a simple message, letter, story or poem.

_____ ☐ 4. Make a working model and demonstrate its operation.

_____ ☐ 5. Build and fly a model airplane or kite.

_____ ☐ 6. Make and play a simple musical instrument.

_____ ☐ 7. Make and use a simple periscope.

_____ ☐ 8. Write a story, skit, poem or limerick.

_____ ☐ 9. Produce an original and imaginative piece of art such as a mobile, sculpture, driftwood article, display of sketches or photographs, picture puzzle, or collage.

_____ ☐ 10. Send and receive a message in code, such as morse code, semaphore or a secret code you made up yourself.

B Requirements

CHECK OFF WHEN COMPLETED AND WRITE THE DATE.

_____ ☐ 1. Tell a story using photographs, slides, video tape, or puppets.

_____ ☐ 2. Make and set up something related to the environment, such as a weather vane, nest box, bird feeder, or composter.

_____ ☐ 3. Paint a mural or do a poster for an event such as Fire Prevention Week, Scoutrees for Canada, Scout-Guide Week, National Wildlife Week or any other special occasion.

_____ ☐ 4. From scrap material, make equipment for games: tetherball equipment, bean bags, rope rings, a slide, swing, trapeze, etc.

_____ ☐ 5. Without hurting nature, make a decorative piece such as a wall plaque, framed picture, lamp shade or lamp stand from a collection of natural articles.

_____ ☐ 6. Recite, sing or perform a skit from a story you have read or written, such as the life of Baden-Powell.

I completed my Tawny Star requirements on:

_____
        (date)

126

Badge Activities

If you enjoyed doing these activities and want to create exciting things, here are some challenging activities you might like to try. These activities can be done by yourself, or with your six, pack, family or friends.

Artist Badge

CHECK OFF WHEN COMPLETED AND WRITE THE DATE.

Do any five of the following:

_____ ☐ 1. Draw or paint an original illustration of an incident or character from a story such as the Jungle Book.

_2010__ ☑ 2. Draw or paint, from life or memory, any animal or person you have seen.

_____ ☐ 3. Draw or paint a landscape while looking at it.

_2009__ ☑ 4. Arrange some items and draw or paint them.

_2009__ ☑ 5. Keep and use a sketch book for a period of one month.

_____ ☐ 6. Illustrate an incident from a story, such as the Jungle Book, using characters in a series of four or more sketches.

_____ ☐ 7. Make a greeting card of your own design.

_____ ☐ 8. Make an original model from any suitable material.

_____ ☐ 9. Create a print using original designs cut into linoleum, potatoes, or other kinds of blocks.

I completed my Artist Badge requirements on:

_____

(date)

Carpenter Badge

CHECK OFF WHEN COMPLETED AND WRITE THE DATE.

With help from an adult, do the following:

_____ ☐ 1. Show the proper and safe use of five basic tools such as: saw, hammer, square, smooth plane, rule and tape measure.

_____ ☐ 2. Show how to take care of basic tools.

Nov. 29 ☑ 3. Using basic tools, construct a project such as a lair divider or curtain, toy storage box, flower box, trinket box, shoe box, model house, tool box, bird house, etc.

_____ ☐ 4. Explain the purpose of the following supplementary tools: hand drill, set of screwdrivers, mitre box, file, wrench, pliers, and vise grip.

_____ ☐ 5. Show how to use two of the supplementary tools.

I completed my Carpenter Badge requirements on:

_____

(date)

Collector Badge

CHECK OFF WHEN COMPLETED AND WRITE THE DATE.

Oct. 17 ☑ Collect and organize a group of objects of your choice and keep your collection for a period of at least three months. Some examples: coins, stamps, photos, books, comics, sports player cards, leaves, matchbox toys, etc. Show and talk about your collection at a pack meeting.

I completed my Collector Badge requirements on:

Oct. 17
(date)

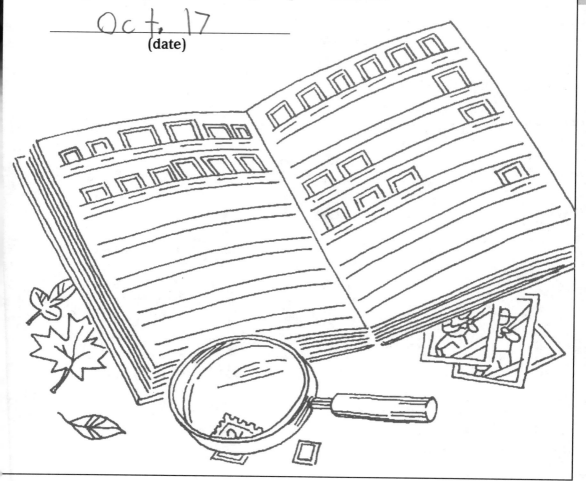

Computer Badge

CHECK OFF WHEN COMPLETED AND WRITE THE DATE.

_____ ☐ 1. From the following list, identify three input devices, three output devices, two storage devices and one processing device. Briefly explain the function of each:

☐ CPU (central processing unit)	☐ Monitor	☐ CD-ROM
	☐ Keyboard	☐ Tape drive
☐ RAM	☐ Hard drive	☐ Scanner
☐ ROM	☐ Mouse	☐ Digital camera
☐ Printer	☐ Joystick	☐ Speakers
☐ Disk drive	☐ Floppy disk	☐ Modem.

_____ ☐ 2. Explain how to care for a computer and disks.

_____ ☐ 3. Do EITHER (a) or (b):
   a) List ten uses of computers in your home and/or school.
   b) Explain how computers are used in entertainment, education and business, or visit a local business, community service or research organization that uses computers, and report on how they use computers in their activities. (Do not use video arcades.)

_____ ☐ 4. a) Briefly explain what the World Wide Web is.
   b) Using the World Wide Web with an adult, find a site that helps you complete requirements for a Cub badge or award. For example, look for a website that has information about star gazing for the Astronomers badge.

_____ ☐ 5. Explain the function of five commands in any computer application.

_____ ☐ 6. Explain to a person who has never used a computer before how to start a computer, open an application, save work, shut down a program and turn off a computer.

_____ ☐ 7. Do EITHER (a) or (b):
   a) Write a story or report using word processing, doing all the revisions on the computer. Print the first draft and the final revision. Explain how you made revisions.
   b) Using a computer, design a new Cub badge or a camp crest. (You may not use clip art.)

I completed my Computer Badge requirements on:

_____

(date)

Entertainer Badge

CHECK OFF WHEN COMPLETED AND WRITE THE DATE.

Do any six of the following:

Date		
2011	☑	1. Play a simple melody on an instrument.
	☐	2. Dress in appropriate costume and act or mime an incident from literature.
2011	☑	3. Perform a recitation.
	☐	4. Sing three songs and lead the pack in singing the chorus.
	☐	5. Lead and sing two folk songs.
	☐	6. Tell a story using puppets.
2011	☑	7. Perform two magic tricks.
	☑	8. Perform a solo dance.
	☐	9. Lead the pack in some form of folk dancing.
2011	☑	10. Direct a group in a skit.
	☐	11. Do a play or dance from the Jungle Book.

I completed my Entertainer Badge requirements on:

_____
(date)

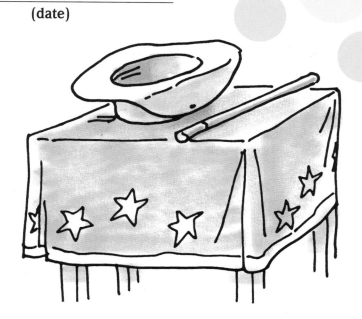

Handicraft Badge

CHECK OFF WHEN COMPLETED AND WRITE THE DATE.

Do any four of the following:

Nov. 28   ☑ 1. Make a toy from recycled odds and ends.

Oct. 17   ☑ 2. Make a toy of some reasonable size, such as a boat, model locomotive, Kub Kar, airplane, animal, etc.

_____   ☐ 3. Make a project such as a farmyard, village, Noah's Ark with animals, Jungle Book scene, cottage with furniture, railroad station, etc.

_____   ☐ 4. Repair two toys. Show them to one of your leaders before and after you work on them.

Nov. 30   ☑ 5. Make two useful or decorative articles from wool, leather, string or other suitable material.

_____   ☐ 6. Build a model kit that takes time and effort to complete.

Nov. 30   ☑ 7. Make a puppet or marionette.

_____   ☐ 8. Make and fly a kite.

I completed my Handicraft Badge requirements on:

Nov. 30

(date)

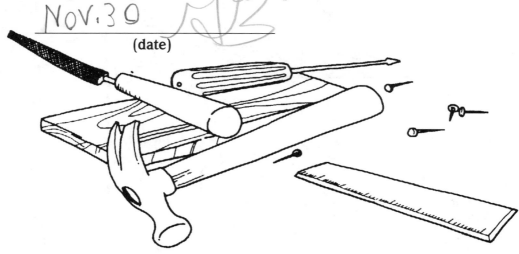

Musician Badge

CHECK OFF WHEN COMPLETED AND WRITE THE DATE.

_____ ☐ 1. Identify the notes of the staff and the values of notes and rest signs.

_____ ☐ 2. Explain the meaning of piano, forte, moderato, staccato, largo, pianissimo, fortissimo.

_____ ☐ 3. Do three of the following:

a) Play a simple tune on a recognized instrument.

b) Demonstrate ability with a rhythm instrument such as castanets, drum, etc.

c) Sing a major scale ascending and descending, and the three notes of a major and minor triad.

d) Tap or clap the rhythm of a four-bar phrase previously played by an adult.

e) Sing a short solo.

f) Be a member of a recognized choir, band or ensemble.

I completed my Musician Badge requirements on:

_____

(date)

Photographer Badge

CHECK OFF WHEN COMPLETED AND WRITE THE DATE.

Can be completed using a camera or video recorder.

A. Do the following:

_____ ☐ 1. Understand and explain the features of the camera you are using and how to properly care for the equipment.

_____ ☐ 2. Explain and demonstrate how to properly load, focus, hold and shoot the camera, along with knowing some common mistakes in taking pictures.

_____ ☐ 3. Understand the different types of film or tape available for your camera and their uses.

B. Using the above skills, complete any three of the following:

_____ ☐ 1. Make a family tree using pictures or video tape.

_____ ☐ 2. Create a display of photographs or video on a subject of your choice.

_____ ☐ 3. Write a short safety story and illustrate it through pictures or video using members of your pack, six or friends as the cast.

_____ ☐ 4. Create a short skit and tell it through photos or video tape using members of your pack, six or friends as the cast.

_____ ☐ 5. Take a set of nature pictures or video and display it to your pack.

_____ ☐ 6. Take a roll of pictures or video of interesting people and places in your community.

_____ ☐ 7. Interview a senior citizen about what life was like at your age using photos or video to record your interview.

_____ ☐ 8. Create a display of photographs or video showing your six or pack at a meeting, outing or camp and show this at a Scouting event.

I completed my Photographer Badge requirements on:

_____

(date)

Reader Badge

CHECK OFF WHEN COMPLETED AND WRITE THE DATE.

_____ ☐ 1. Do any two of the following:
   a) With adult help, make up a list of books that might interest you and read three of them.
   b) Discuss with an adult what you think were the main features of a book you read.
   c) Tell or read to your pack, your six or a small group a story or part of a story you have read.

_____ ☐ 2. Do any two of the following:
   a) Show your ability to use the local school or public library by explaining its rules and the reasons for them. Explain the use of the card, microfiche, or computer catalogue and describe, in general terms, the locations of the different categories of books.
   b) Be a member of the local library and hold a library card.
   c) Show how to use a dictionary, atlas and an encyclopedia.

_____ ☐ 3. Do any two of the following:
   a) Describe the parts of a book: table of contents, foreword, chapters, glossary, index, etc.
   b) Show how to open a new book and how to care for all books.
   c) Make and title a dust-cover for a book.

_____ ☐ 4. Read a story from the Jungle Book and retell it to your six or pack.

_____ ☐ 5. With adult help, select a children's book and read it aloud to a Beaver or other young child.

I completed my Reader Badge requirements on:

_____

   (date)

Canadian Arts Award

If you love being creative and want more challenge, try working on these activities. These activities can be done by yourself, or with your six, pack, family or friends.

CHECK OFF WHEN COMPLETED AND WRITE THE DATE.

To achieve this award, you must complete the following:

_____ ☐ 1. Earn the Tawny Star.
_2011_ ☑ 2. Earn one of the Creative Expression related badges.
_2011_ ☑ 3. Visit with an artisan, craftsman, author, musician, or serious hobbyist and learn about their work or activities.
_2010_ ☑ 4. Participate in a cultural event such as an art or craft show, concert, play, choir, or community performance.

I completed my Canadian Arts Award requirements on:

_____
(date)

This Award may be worn on your Scout sash after you become a Scout.

Helicopter

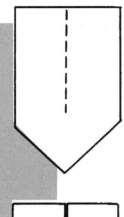

You need:

- Stiff paper or thin cardboard (a file card is good)
- A cork
- A rounded toothpick, or a 3.75 cm (1 1/2 inch) nail, or a burned wooden match
- Scissors
- Tape

How to make it:

1. Cut the paper or cardboard to look like this.
2. Tape the toothpick, nail, or match to the shape.
3. Bend your shape like this.
4. Push the stick into the cork. If you are using a wooden match, push very carefully so that it won't break. Try making a hole, smaller than your stick, in the cork first.
5. Take your helicopter outside and throw it into the air. You can even do it inside if the room is big enough and you are sure that you won't break anything.

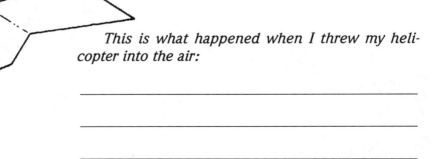

This is what happened when I threw my helicopter into the air:

_____

_____

_____

_____

A Paddle Boat

You need:

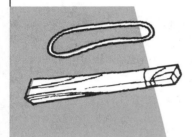

1. A small piece of plywood 6 mm thick, about 5 cm wide, and 8 cm long
2. Two pieces of wood 18 mm thick, 18 mm wide and 12 cm long
3. Some coated cardboard from a milk carton
4. Small nails
5. One or two elastic bands about 5 cm long

How to make it:

1. Cut the ends of the two pieces of wood on a diagonal, and put them together as shown in the diagram. The two nails at the back should stick out a bit so that they will hold the elastic.

2. From the milk carton, cut two pieces 7.5 cm long and 2.5 cm wide. In the centre of each, cut notches half-way across so that you can fit them together to make a paddle wheel.

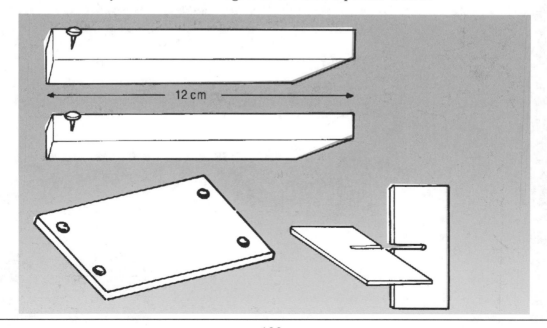

12 cm

3. Cut squares of cardboard 2.5 cm by 2.5 cm. Fold them in half and staple them into the middle of the paddle wheel to strengthen it.

4. Mount the paddle wheel on the back of your boat using the elastic and two nails as shown in the first diagram.

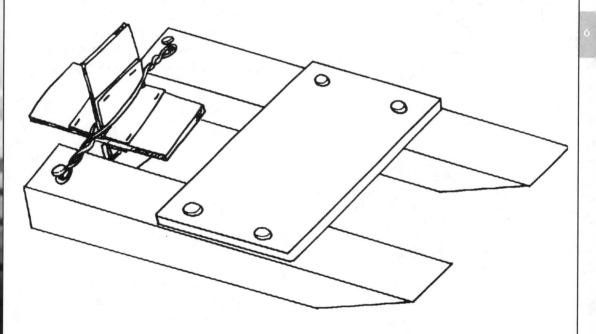

I sailed my paddle boat _____

(where)

and it worked just _____ .

An Easy Kite

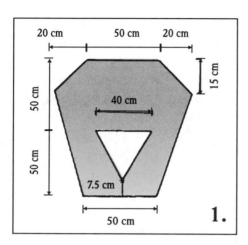

1.

You need:

1. A piece of polyethylene plastic 100 cm long and 90 cm wide. The best is 200 gauge polyethylene from a hardware store, but you can also use a strong garbage bag.

2. Two spars 95 cm long and 6 mm thick. Bamboo garden canes split length-wise down the middle will do, or you can buy thin mouldings from a hardware or building supplies store.

3. Plastic tape at least 3.75 cm wide

4. Kite line or other thin string

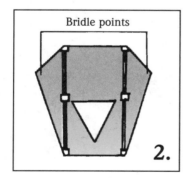

Bridle points

2.

How to make it:

1. Measure and cut the plastic carefully.

2. Lay spars on the kite and tape down. Notice where the middle points are for the next step.

3. Strengthen the bridle points on the plastic by putting tape on both sides.

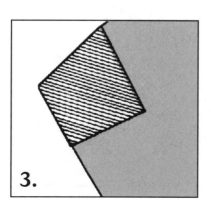

3.

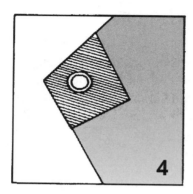

4

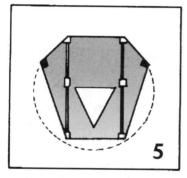

5

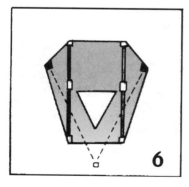

6

4. Punch a hole at each bridle point. If you can, strengthen the holes with metal eyelets.

5. Tie a string 3.6 m long between the holes for your bridle.

6. Tie a loop in the *exact* centre of your bridle.

7. Attach the flying string to the loop.

8. Take out your kite on a breezy day and let it go!

Note: This type of kite, known as a sled kite, can deflate if hit by a sudden sidewind. They are best flown in a steady breeze.

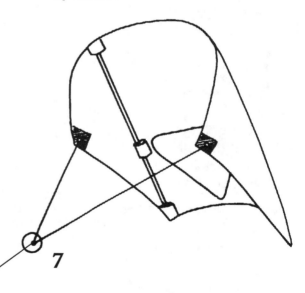

7

This is how long and high I flew my kite:

(Time)	(Height)

Computer-type Circuits

Circuits in computers are on very small chips about the size of your fingernail. In fact, there can be many circuits on one chip. This project will help you understand what a circuit or a chip does. They make either "And" or "Or" types of choices. Try building your own circuits to see how this works.

"AND" and "OR" Circuits

"AND" Condition
To light the bulb
Switch 1 AND
Switch 2 must
be closed.

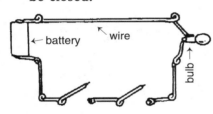

"OR" Condition
To light the bulb,
Switch 1 OR Switch
2 must be closed.

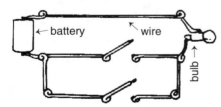

You need:

1. Two dozen clean finishing nails (used as switches)
2. One piece 30.5 cm x 30.5 cm plywood
3. 1.2 m light wire (wire must be bare wherever it makes contact with battery, bulb or other pieces of wire)
4. Masking or electrician's tape (to hold wire in contact with battery and bulb)
5. One size "D" battery
6. One flashlight bulb

"AND" and "OR" Conditions

For a bigger challenge, try making a circuit that combines "AND" and "OR" decisions. When all switches are closed, the bulb lights up to show the circuit is successfully completed.

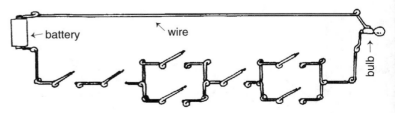

A Barometer

Did you make the rain gauge shown in Chapter 4? Here is another weather instrument you can try.

You need:

1. A large wide-mouth jar, like a peanut butter jar
2. A balloon
3. Rubber bands
4. A drinking straw
5. Tape
6. Stiff paper or cardboard

How to make it:

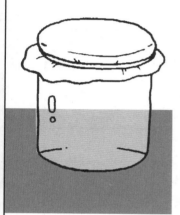

1. Wash the jar. Discard the lid.
2. Cut a piece of balloon larger than the mouth of the glass jar.
3. Stretch the balloon smoothly and tightly over the mouth of the jar. Hold it in place with rubber bands.
4. Carefully cut the ends of the straw diagonally, so that they are pointed. Tape one end of the straw to the centre of the balloon. The straw will be the pointer.
5. Fold the paper or cardboard to make a long triangular tube that will stand by itself. Hold it together with tape.
6. Stand the jar on a flat surface away from sources of heat such as a radiator, stove, or sunlight.
7. Stand the tube near, but not quite touching, the end of your pointer. Make a mark on the tube at the tip of the pointer and write down what the weather is like (sunny, cloudy, stormy) beside the mark. Once or twice a day, make a mark on your tube and write down what the weather is like.

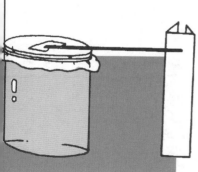

8. After a few days, you should find that the weather is usually sunny when the pointer moves toward the top of the tube and cloudy or stormy when the pointer moves towards the bottom of the tube.

A barometer measures changes in air pressure. When the pressure goes down, the weather turns cloudy: when the pressure goes up, the weather usually clears.

My Barometer Record		
Time of Day Twice a day	Pointer Up/Down	Weather Sunny/Cloudy
1		
1		
2		
2		
3		
3		
4		
4		
5		
5		

A Bass Fiddle

Do you like music? You and your friends can form your own band using instruments you have made yourself. Start with a bass fiddle.

You need:

1. A big cardboard box
2. A broom handle or some other long pole
3. Strong string about 1.5 metres long
4. A short stick

How to make it:

1. Punch a small hole in the bottom of the box.
2. Push one end of the string through the hole and tie it to the short stick. The stick should be inside the box.
3. Tie the other end of the string to the broom.
4. Rest the broom handle on the box and brace it with one foot. Hold the handle with one hand so that the string is tight, and pluck the string with your other hand. You can change the note you play by moving the broom to tighten the string.

This is the song I played:

_____

I thought it sounded:

6

145

A Glass Xylophone

You need:

1. At least eight drinking glasses all the same size. You can use more if you can get them.
2. A wooden spoon
3. Water

How to make it:

1. Fill each glass with a different amount of water. Set the glasses in a row with the fullest glass to your left and the emptiest to your right.

2. Starting on your left, tap each glass with the spoon. Notice that each glass rings a different note.

3. Experiment by pouring water in and out of the glasses until you can play a "do-re-me" scale on the glasses OR invent your own scale if you like.

4. If you have two wooden spoons, you can play chords by tapping two glasses at once. Which chords sound best?

I played this song: _____

and it sounded just _____

Maracas

Maracas are easy to make and fun to experiment with. You need a small container with a lid you can close tightly and something you can put into the container to shake. Plastic food holders, soft drink cans with tape over the opening or small cardboard boxes taped shut make good containers. Try popping corn, dried beans or other seeds, small pebbles, or even small screws or nuts and bolts as shakers.

Experiment with different containers and different shakers to see what sounds you get from each. The shape of your container will also make a big difference in the rhythm of the sound.

If you make lots of different kinds of maracas, you will come across one or two that you can shake in many different rhythms to make a really good sound. These are the ones you want to keep for your band.

I made my maracas out of:

_____

and they looked like this:

Other Musical Instruments

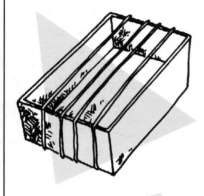

There is almost no limit to the different musical instruments you can make. Here are some more ideas. Check those that you try.

☐ With their bowls back-to-back, hold two dessert spoons loosely between the fingers of one hand. Hold your other hand over your knee and rattle the spoons between your hand and knee.

☐ Make a cigar-box banjo by stretching different size elastic bands over the open side of a small wooden box.

☐ Make a drum by stretching a piece of rubber or leather tightly over a large tin can.

☐ Check your school or community library for books on making simple instruments.

After you have made an instrument or two, you and your friends can play along with the songs on the radio, a record, or a tape, and make up a small band. When you think that you sound pretty good, take your instruments to Cubs and play for the pack.

We named our band _____

The Cubs in my band were:

_____

_____

_____

_____

We played these songs for the pack:

_____

_____

_____

_____

This is how the other Cubs reacted:

_____

_____

_____

Skits

There are other kinds of things you can make, too. Have you ever made up a story, poem, or skit? A skit is especially fun to do because you can work on it with your friends and have everybody share ideas about how it should go. Make sure that each of you has a part.

Skits are great around the campfire, but you can do them at pack meetings or Parent and Cub banquets, on outings, after lunch, or any time the pack needs some entertainment. The easiest way to make up a skit is to use one that's already been done and change it around to suit yourselves. One of your leaders or other Cubs can probably suggest ideas, because there are hundreds of skits going around in Cubs and Scouts. Some of them are very old: your parents and grandparents probably acted them out when they were young.

If you want to make up an original skit, try one of these ideas.

1. **Bus or Airplane Trip:** Passengers make comments on the scenery and lean over or bounce around according to the travel conditions.

2. **Restaurant:** Diners order crazy food combinations. Waiter gets them mixed up.

3. **Newspaper Office:** Reporters rush in with new stories. Editor accepts or rejects them for printing.

4. **Star Gazing:** Astronomers search the sky with telescopes and report on what they see.

5. **Wild Dreams:** Players come on one by one and act out what they dreamed last night.

6. **Secret Wishes:** Players whisper their wishes to a magician, and then go behind a screen and come out with their wishes granted. Magician comments on what is happening.

When you act in a skit, you can be a real ham! Use extra big gestures and make the characters you are playing show their emotions clearly. Acting in a skit is a perfect chance to let yourself go, have lots of fun, and really become the character you are playing!

Ask Akela to make some time for skits at one of your Cub meetings. Then you and your friends can go to work to plan your performance.

Here is a description of my favourite skit and the part I played in it:

_____

_____

_____

_____

_____

_____

_____

_____

_____

Some special things I learned are:

_____

_____

_____

_____

_____

_____

Some things I'd like to try next time:

_____

_____

_____

_____

Some things I'd like to try when I get to Scouts:

_____

_____

_____

_____

_____

CHAPTER 7

The Health and Fitness

Activity Area

veryone is different. Some of us are good in sports and some are good at other things. Some of us never seem to get sick while others have to spend a lot of time in bed or in the hospital. Whoever we are, we want to look after and develop ourselves as well as we can. This chapter will give you some ideas on how to be fit and healthy and have some fun while you're doing it.

Red Star Activities

No matter who you are, having an active life is the first step in being fit and healthy. These activities will teach you the basics of how to take care of your body and keep it in shape.

To earn the Red Star, choose and do any five of the A requirements and any two of the B requirements. These activities can be done by yourself, or with your six, pack, family or friends.

A Requirements

CHECK OFF WHEN COMPLETED AND WRITE THE DATE.

_____ ☐ 1. Choose and do any five of the stretching activities illustrated in this chapter (Pages 173, 174).

_____ ☐ 2. Develop and follow your own personal Active Living Program, with at least 15 minutes per day of actvity for a two week period.

_____ ☐ 3. Describe some safety rules for water activities.

_____ ☐ 4. Lead a group in an active game and explain why good sportsmanship is important.

_____ ☐ 5. Discuss how to protect your body from injury in different sports, such as using eye protectors, mouth guard, helmets or padding.

_____ ☐ 6. Show the proper way to sit, stand, walk, and run. Learn how to take your pulse rate before and after exercise.

_____ ☐ 7. Plan balanced meals for home or camp.

_____ ☐ 8. Describe the dangers of the common cold and explain three ways to prevent it from spreading.

_____ ☐ 9. Describe how to take care of your own clothing and belongings and explain why such care is important.

_____ ☐ 10. Describe how to take care of your hair, ears, eyes, teeth, nose, nails and feet, and explain why. Explain the importance of washing your hands before handling food, before eating, and after using the washroom.

B Requirements

CHECK OFF WHEN COMPLETED AND WRITE THE DATE.

_____ ☐ 1. Meet with a health worker or other knowledgeable adult to discuss, or make a display showing the effects tobacco use has on your body.

_____ ☐ 2. Meet with a health worker, police officer or other knowledgeable adult to discuss, or make a display showing the effects alcohol and drug abuse have on your body.

_____ ☐ 3. Design, build and use a simple gym or an outdoor obstacle course.

I completed my Red Star requirements on:

_____
(date)

Badge Activities

If you enjoy being active, here are some more challenging activities you can try out. These activities can be done by yourself, or with your six, pack, family or friends.

Athlete Badge

CHECK OFF WHEN COMPLETED AND WRITE THE DATE.

_____ ☐ 1. Show the proper way to sit, stand, walk, and run. Learn how to take your pulse rate before and after exercise.

_____ ☐ 2. Explain to an adult and your six the importance of diet, sleep, and exercise to the development of your body.

_____ ☐ 3. Take part in an ongoing personal fitness program. Explain the importance of warmup and cool down exercises.

_____ ☐ 4. Demonstrate your best in any seven (7) of the following:
   a) a 50 metre run
   b) a 200 metre run
   c) a running high jump
   d) a running long jump
   e) a standing long jump
   f) sit-ups
   g) push-ups
   h) a rope or pole climb
   i) a baseball or frisbee throw
   j) a long distance run
   k) rope skipping

I completed my Athlete Badge requirements on:

2011
_____
(date)

Cyclist Badge

CHECK OFF WHEN COMPLETED AND WRITE THE DATE.

_____ ☐ 1. Own or have access to, and use an approved bicycling helmet while earning this badge. Explain how to tell if a helmet is approved for bicycling.

Jan. 10 ☑ 2. Have the use of a bicycle that is the right size for you and conduct the following safety check:
   a) Check lights, reflectors, pedals, seat, horn or bell for good working condition
   b) Check handle grips for tightness
   c) Check steering assembly for tightness
   d) Check tires for air pressure and cuts
   e) Check all nuts and bolts for tightness
   f) Check chain for tightness and properly oil the chain
   g) Check wheels for wobbles and broken spokes
   h) Show how to keep the bike clean

_____ ☐ 3. Explain the meaning of the following street signs or signals and how to properly respond.
   a) Stop sign
   b) Yield sign
   c) Pedestrian crosswalk sign
   d) Colours of a traffic light
   e) Railway crossing sign
   f) One way sign

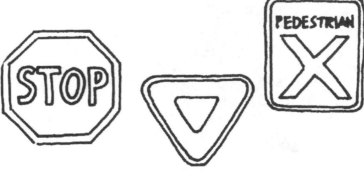

_____ ☐ 4. In a safe, off-road area, demonstrate
the following skills:
   a) Start, stop and pedal smoothly
   b) Ride in a straight line
   c) Do a shoulder check: while riding in a straight line, look back over your shoulder for a few seconds. Be able to ride in a straight line while looking back and tell your leader what you saw.
   d) Hand signals for left turn, right turn and stop.

_____ ☐ 5. Explain why you should stop and check for traffic before riding out of your driveway and know what side of the road to ride on.

_____ ☐ 6. Explain how to make yourself more visible at night by wearing bright and reflective clothing, use of bike reflectors and lights.

_____ ☐ 7. Explain other bicycling safety tips such as riding in wet weather, avoiding road hazards such as holes and grates, avoiding car doors, and how to lock your bike.

_____ ☐ 8. To be done after other items have been completed. With the help of an adult, choose a safe route to bike in your neighbourhood. Bike for 10 minutes on this safe route with an adult. Explain how riding your bike (as opposed to using a car) for 10 minutes is good for the environment.

I completed my Cyclist Badge requirements on:

2 0 1 1

_____
(date)

SCOUTS CANADA

CLIMATE CHANGE CHALLENGE
DÉFI CHANGEMENT CLIMATIQUE

(See page 259)

Skater Badge

(ice, roller skates
or in-line skates)

CHECK OFF WHEN COMPLETED AND WRITE THE DATE.

_____ ☐ 1. Know and discuss the safety rules for skating. For ice skating, include ice safety. For roller skating and in-line skating, include street safety and use of protective gear such as helmet, pads and gloves.

_____ ☐ 2. Show how to care for your skating equipment.

_____ ☐ 3. Demonstrate how to start and stop on a given signal. Then demonstrate any five of the following moves:
- a) Skate forward with arms free or behind body.
- b) Skate backward.
- c) Make turns to left and right, cutting corners.
- d) Skate in a curve counter-clockwise.
- e) Glide on one skate for three metres.
- f) Forward and back edges on alternate feet on curves not less than five metres.
- g) Forward cross cuts, clockwise and counter-clockwise, on a circle three metres in diameter.
- h) Back cross cuts, clockwise and counter-clock-wise, on a circle three metres in diameter.
- i) Two jumps with clean and controlled landings.
- j) A simple spin on two feet.

I completed my Skater Badge requirements on:

$\underline{\text{2 8 11}}$

(date)

Skier Badge

(downhill and
cross-country)

CHECK OFF WHEN COMPLETED AND WRITE THE DATE.

_____ ☐ 1. Show how to carry poles and skis properly.
_____ ☐ 2. Show how to care for your equipment properly, including how to store it off-season.
_____ ☐ 3. Explain some rules for safety when skiing.
_____ ☐ 4. Put on your own skis and adjust the bindings properly.
_____ ☐ 5. Climb a hill using side-step, traverse and herringbone.
_____ ☐ 6. Snowplow straight down a hill in complete control.
_____ ☐ 7. Do right and left linked snowplow turns.
_____ ☐ 8. Describe how to get help in case of a skiing accident.
_____ ☐ 9. Explain how to dress for various types of weather.
_____ ☐ 10. Do EITHER (a) or (b):
　　　　　　　　　　　a) Show the safe use of a rope tow, T-Bar, or chair lift.
　　　　　　　　　　　b) Describe the emergency equipment and supplies you should carry on a cross-country ski trip.

I completed my Skier Badge requirements on:

_____
　　　　　(date)

Snowboarder Badge

CHECK OFF WHEN COMPLETED AND WRITE THE DATE.

_____ ☐ 1. Show how to care for your board and boots, and how to put them on properly. (This should include the use of a "runaway strap" or a "leash.")

_____ ☐ 2. Demonstrate how to mount and dismount either a surface lift (rope tow, T-bar, poma and platter) or a chairlift — whichever is used on beginner and intermediate hills in your area.

_____ ☐ 3. Explain proper dress, including the use of a helmet, when in snowboarding parks or half pipes.

_____ ☐ 4. Demonstrate your ability to do the following:

☐ Walking/skating   ☐ Traverse with a stop
☐ Climbing side stepping   ☐ Static rotation exercise
☐ Straight running   ☐ Isolated beginner turns
   (toe/heel drag)   ☐ Linked beginner turns

_____ ☐ 5. Know and understand the Alpine Responsibility Code:

Alpine Responsibility Code
This Code applies to all alpine skiers and snowboarders using alpine ski slopes.

Every skier or snowboarder must:

a. Obey the signs.

b. Yield the right of way to skiers or snowboarders downhill, and choose a course that does not jeopardize their safety.

c. Yield the right of way to skiers or snowboarders uphill when entering a slope, and at intersections.

d. Use skis equipped with safety edges and a braking system.

e. Make sure, when stopping on a slope, that you are visible to skiers or snowboarders uphill, and that you are not obstructing the slope.

Skiers or snowboarders must not:

a. Make a fast downhill run.

b. Make jumps.

c. Ski or snowboard outside the ski slopes.

d. Ski or snowboard on a closed slope.

e. Ski or snowboard while wearing a portable player (ie. Discman™).

f. Cross the track of a surface ski lift in operation.

g. Remove any signs.

h. Leave the site of an accident in which you are involved without identifying yourself to a first aider.

I completed my Snowboarder Badge requirements on:

_____

(date)

Swimmer Badge

Hold the Canadian Red Cross Swim Kids Level 7/ Aqua Quest Level 7 or Life-saving Society's Swimmer 4 award or do the following:

CHECK OFF WHEN COMPLETED AND WRITE THE DATE.

_____ ☐ 1. Explain and show how to use the buddy system.
_____ ☐ 2. Show how to check a swimming area for possible dangers, such as deep water, rocks, and slippery surfaces.
_____ ☐ 3. Complete all of the following:
   a) Tread water in deep water (over your head) for a minimum of 1½ minutes.
   b) Enter the water using the front dive (the stride position).
   c) Front crawl 25 metres.
   d) Back crawl 25 metres.
   e) Endurance swim 75 metres.

I completed my Swimmer Badge requirements on:

_____
(date)

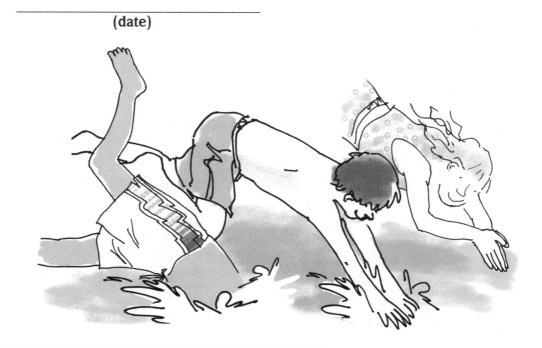

Team Player Badge

CHECK OFF WHEN COMPLETED AND WRITE THE DATE.

Oct. 17 ☑ 1. Be a regular member of an organized sport team. The team must be under the supervision of a Cub leader or other approved person.

_____ ☑ 2. Explain the basic rules of the sport you play.

_____ ☑ 3. Take part in at least six games.

_____ ☑ 4. Show a good sportsman-like spirit in all Cub games and activities.

I completed my Team Player Badge requirements on:

_____
(date)

The Canadian Healthy Living Award

Do you really enjoy being active? Are you ready for a real challenge? If so, try these activities. You're sure to become healthy and fit while discovering more interesting facts and fun. These activities can be done by yourself, or with your six, pack, family or friends.

CHECK OFF WHEN COMPLETED AND WRITE THE DATE.

To achieve this award, you must complete the following:

_____ ☐ 1. Earn the Red Star.

_2010_ ☑ 2. Earn one of the Health and Fitness related badges.

_2011_ ☑ 3. Earn two of the Outdoor Activity related badges.

_2011_ ☑ 4. Participate in a hike-a-thon, bike-a-thon, special runs or some other activity that creates public awareness for being fit and healthy.

_____ ☐ 5. Create a display or participate in a program based on some of the Olympic sports.

_____ ☐ 6. Research and report on a Canadian outdoor person or sports figure who has made significant contributions to Canada or the world.

_____ ☐ 7. Help show other Cubs how to safely participate in a physical activity of your choice.

I completed my Canadian Healthy Living Award requirements on:

_____

(date)

This Award may be worn on your Scout sash after you become a Scout.

Keeping Clean

You've probably learned about cleanliness at home or in school. Just to remind you, here are some simple ways to help yourself keep clean and away from germs that might make you sick. After you've read them, put down the book and see how many you can remember.

Hair

- Wash your hair regularly and after active sports or a dirty job.
- To prevent the spread of head lice, use your own brush and comb. Do not wear another person's hat.

Eyes

- Keep your fingers away from your eyes.
- Wash your face when you wake in the morning and before you go to bed.

Ears

- Never put anything sharp into your ears.
- Wash them every day.
- If you have trouble hearing or your ear aches, tell your parents.

Nose

- Try not to blow your nose too hard. It can damage your ear passages because they are connected to your nose.
- Keep your fingers out of your nose so that you won't catch germs that can cause a cold.
- Use a tissue or clean handkerchief to wipe your nose.

Mouth

- Brush your teeth after every meal and after you eat sweets and other sticky things.
- Floss your teeth daily.
- If you can't brush after a meal, rinse out your mouth with water.
- Do not share your toothbrush.
- Cover your mouth when you sneeze to prevent the spread of germs.

Hands

- Wash your hands before eating or touching food.
- Wash your hands after using the toilet, and after handling animals.

Nails

- Cut your finger nails and toe nails with a clipper before they get too long.

Feet

- Wash your feet regularly.
- Wear clean socks every day.
- Wear proper footwear for the weather (e.g. snow boots for winter).

General

- Bathe or shower daily, particularly after working up a good sweat.
- Change your underwear daily.
- Keep your room and belongings clean and tidy.

Did you remember all the ways to keep clean and avoid germs? If you weren't sure of some of them, read them over and test yourself again.

This is what I already do well:

_____

_____

_____

_____

This is what I want to do better:

_____

_____

_____

7

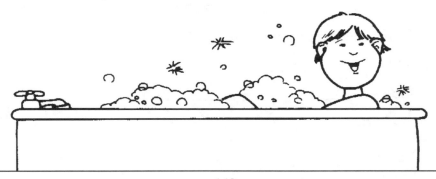

Good Food and Cooking

Have you ever seen Canada's Food Guide to Healthy Eating? The food guide helps you choose different kinds of food to eat so that your body gets enough of the good things it needs to grow as well as it can.

Ask your parents to let you choose some of your family's meals by using the food rainbow from Canada's Food Guide. It shows four types of food that you should eat every day. These groups are milk products; grain products; meat and alternatives; and vegetables and fruit. When you eat food from all four groups every day, you have a good balanced diet.

Look at the food chart, then list your favourite foods from each of the four groups.

Scource: Canada's Food Guide to Healthy Eating, http://www.hc-sc.gc.ca/fn-an/ alt_formats/hpfb-dgpsa/pdf/food-guide-aliment/fg_rainbow_bw-arc_en_ciel_ga_nb_e.pdf, Health Canada, 1997, Reproduced with the permission of the Minister of Public Works and Government Services Canada, 2006. Please note that Canada's Food Guide to Healthy Eating is being revised. The current target date is Fall 2006.

My favourite foods from each group are:

Milk products: _____

Grain products: _____

Meat and alternatives: _____

Vegetables and fruit: _____

And while you're at it, ask your parents to let you do some of the cooking, too. With your parents' help, you can cook lots of things. You can fry an egg, make a dessert, or just heat up something out of a can. Food that you've helped to cook tastes best. After cooking and eating, remember to help with the clean up. It's always easier if everyone shares the work.

These are my three favourite meals:

_____

_____

_____

_____

Here is my own special recipe:

_____

_____

_____

_____

_____

_____

7

Exercise

To keep your body healthy, you need exercise. You probably get lots of exercise when you play active games with your friends. It's a good idea to get into the habit of exercising now, so that you can easily keep it up as you grow older. Here are hints to help you exercise.

The best way to keep fit is to build exercise into the things you do every day. When you go somewhere, for example, walk or ride your bike whenever you can.

Be active, especially outdoors, for part of every day when you play with your friends. Street hockey, rope skipping, relay races, tobogganing, obstacle courses, and tag games are always lots of fun. Go on outings with your pack, family and friends. Hikes, camping, swimming, snowshoeing and cross-country skiing are great things to do to stay fit.

Lower back stretch

Play a team sport such as soccer, softball, or hockey, where you have to be alert and move around a lot. Try to avoid sports that have a lot of crunching body contact. Your body is developing and doesn't need to be bumped, banged and bruised on purpose.

If you are going to do some physical exercise, warm up first by stretching your body and muscles. One of your leaders or your teachers may be able to help you choose a set of warm-up exercises. They will help you loosen up so you don't strain muscles. Your body is like plasticine. It's easier to work with when you warm it up. Try these stretching exercises before starting any physical activity. Each stretch should be held for about 20 seconds.

Hamstring stretch

- **Achilles tendon and calf muscle stretch (wall push-ups)**

- **Quadracep stretch**

- **Hamstring stretch**

- **Lower back stretch**

- **Arm and side stretch**

Quadracep stretch

Achilles tendon and calf muscle stretch (wall push-ups)

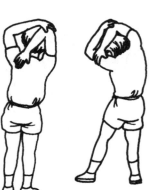

Arm and side stretch

Groin stretch

Hurdle stretch

- **Groin stretch**

- **Hurdle stretch**

After your activity, your muscles may feel tight. Take a few minutes to cool down and do the stretching exercises again to keep your muscles loose and flexible.

To see if your body has been working hard during exercises, it's useful to take your pulse rate before and after the activity. While resting, put your hand on your heart or on the side of your neck and count the number of heartbeats in a minute. Then take your pulse right after you exercise. You'll be able to see how hard your heart and body are working to stay fit and healthy. The faster your heart beats, the harder you've been working.

	Before Exercise	*After Exercise*
My Pulse rate is:	_____	_____

(heartbeats per minute)

These are new kinds of exercises I'd like to try:

Exercise	*Who can help*	*When I did them*

Ask your parents or an adult friend to help you make some simple exercise equipment. Here are two ideas you can use. Make sure that you test all equipment for safety before you use it. Then, take or draw a picture of the equipment you've made and show it to your six. Better yet, invite your six over to try it out.

Back Yard Gym

You can put together this simple gym if you have a large sturdy tree in your yard or can arrange to have a large pole solidly placed in the ground.

In your basement, you can anchor many of these devices to the joists under your ceiling with eye bolts and hook arrangements that allow you to remove them when you're not using them. Be sure to put good padding, like an old mattress, on the floor to protect you.

Muscle Builder

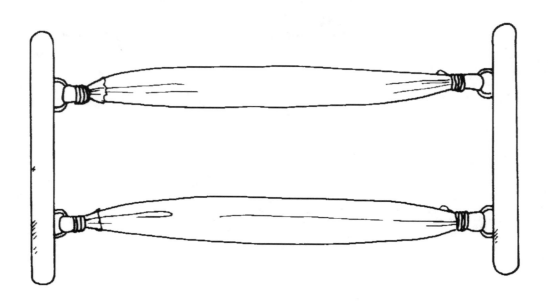

You can make this from easy-to-get material. It helps to build shoulder and arm muscles.

You need:

1. Two pieces of dowel 35 cm long and 2.5 to 3 cm in diameter (a broom handle will do)

2. Four eye bolts long enough to go through the dowels

3. Two pieces of old bicycle inner tube, each about 50 cm long

4. String or tape to fasten tubing to the eye bolts

Obstacle Course

Ask a leader to help you and your six run an outdoor obstacle course for the pack. Have a meeting with your six and decide what equipment each Cub will bring. Here are some ideas to try.

❑ Walk a 3 to 5 metre length of 5 cm x 10 cm stud or a 15 cm plank set on edge in the ground.
❑ Toss a ball or stone into a bucket 3 metres away.
❑ Climb through a tire suspended from a tree.
❑ Crawl under a bench or board set 30 cm off the ground.
❑ Swing on a rope from one spot to another.
❑ Walk on stilts for 3 metres.
❑ Climb up a 3 metre rope, pole or tree.
❑ Walk for 3 to 6 metres along a series of 750 mL cans set 30 cm apart.
❑ Climb over a chest-high barricade made from picnic tables set on their sides.
❑ Crawl under a 3 x 4 metre tarpaulin that has been pegged down.
❑ Run through a speed race area.
❑ Do a headstand or cartwheel.
❑ Climb through a barrel open at both ends.

It's best to set up your obstacles in a large circle so that you can move quickly from one to another.

You can even run your obstacle course in the winter by building lots of obstacles out of snow.

Remember to exercise every day if you can. Regular exercise is a habit to keep all your life.

Bicycle Safety

Bike riding is great fun when it is done safely. If you use a bike, you should know how to care for it and ride it properly. Here are some things you should know and practice.

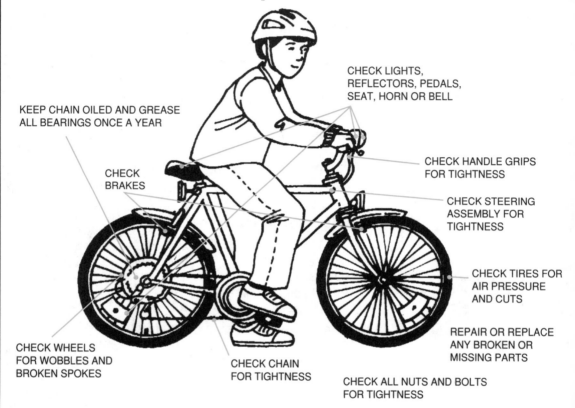

CHECK LIGHTS, REFLECTORS, PEDALS, SEAT, HORN OR BELL

KEEP CHAIN OILED AND GREASE ALL BEARINGS ONCE A YEAR

CHECK HANDLE GRIPS FOR TIGHTNESS

CHECK BRAKES

CHECK STEERING ASSEMBLY FOR TIGHTNESS

CHECK TIRES FOR AIR PRESSURE AND CUTS

REPAIR OR REPLACE ANY BROKEN OR MISSING PARTS

CHECK WHEELS FOR WOBBLES AND BROKEN SPOKES

CHECK CHAIN FOR TIGHTNESS

CHECK ALL NUTS AND BOLTS FOR TIGHTNESS

Bike Check

Before riding your bike, check it over to make sure it is in good shape. The Cyclist Badge has a check list you can use.

I checked my bike and found these things needed fixing:

_____

_____

Road Signs

Riding a bike is like driving a car. You must obey all traffic rules and signs. Ask your parents or leaders to help you learn what each one of these signs and signals mean.

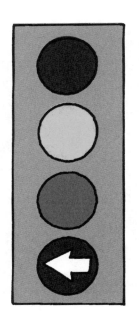

- Stop signs
- Yield
- Crossovers
- One way - Traffic can move in one direction only (shown by the arrow)
- Railway Crossing - Be very careful when you see this sign. It tells you that there are train tracks nearby. Remember, it's easier for you to stop than it is for the train to stop! Now, carefully look left, look right, then look left again. If the way is clear, you can WALK YOUR BIKE ACROSS THE TRACKS!
- Red light - Means you must bring your bike to a full stop.
- Amber light - Means you must bring your bike to a full stop if you can, because the red light is about to appear!
- Green light - Means you may move ahead if the intersection is clear. When you're turning on a GREEN light, remember the pedestrians have the right of way.
- Arrows - Means you may enter the intersection to move only in the direction shown by the arrow.

Ride Safely

To keep safe while riding, know these hand signals.

This is the compulsory signalling code:

left turn

right turn

slowing down or stopping

Safety Tips

While you are riding, remember these rules and always follow them.

WOLF CUBS ALWAYS:
- Wear an approved bike helmet.
- Drive their bikes in the same direction as traffic, on the right hand side of the road, single file.
- Use the correct hand signals when they want to turn, slow down or stop.
- Obey all traffic rules, signs and lights.
- Keep both hands on the handlebar, except when they are signalling.
- Walk their bikes across busy intersections.
- Wear light coloured or reflective clothing at night, and make sure their bikes have the correct safety equipment.
- Stop and look left, then right, then left again before entering traffic from a driveway or lane.
- Watch for road obstacles like sewer grates, bumps or potholes.
- Use bicycle paths when they are provided.
- Record their bike's complete description and even have it engraved with an identifying mark. This makes the bike easier to identify if it gets found after being stolen.
- Carefully lock their bike to a solid object.
- Are very careful of parked cars, because the drivers could suddenly open their doors in their path.

WOLF CUBS NEVER:

- Ride two on a bike.
- Race with each other, with cars, trucks or buses.
- Attach carts or any objects to their bikes.
- Weave in and out of traffic.
- Perform stunts.
- Carry parcels in their hands while driving their bicycles.
- Wear headphones or listen to portable stereos when driving their bikes. (You must always be able to hear other traffic, fire trucks, ambulances, police cars, and even other Wolf Cubs!)
- Ride their bikes on the sidewalk unless designated as an official bicycle path.
- Leave their bikes lying on the ground where someone could fall over them.

Drugs and Their Effect on the Body

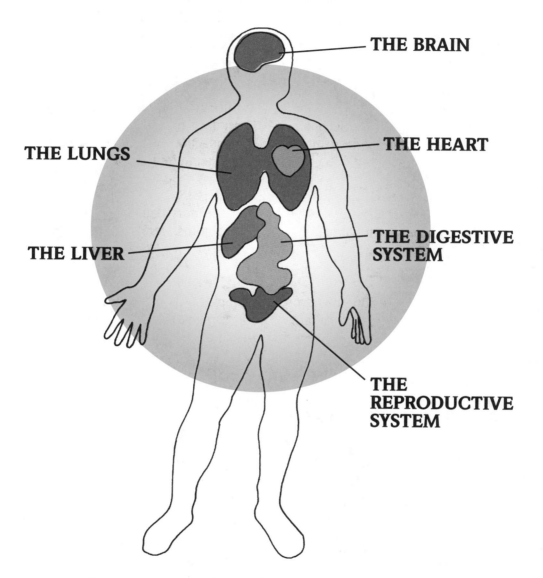

THE BRAIN

THE HEART

THE LUNGS

THE LIVER

THE DIGESTIVE SYSTEM

THE REPRODUCTIVE SYSTEM

7

Smart people do not hurt themselves on purpose. Taking drugs is just plain dumb because it hurts your mind and body. When you really think about it, taking drugs is not very cool. Be yourself and say NO to drugs.

Here's how different drugs can hurt you.

DRUGS AND THEIR EFFECT ON THE BODY

THE BRAIN
marijuana, LSD, PCP, Mescaline or Peyote, Psilocybin, STP or DOM, PMA, opium, Seconal, alcohol, valium, benzedrine, cocaine, tobacco, caffeine

Effects
memory or concentration difficulties, depression, anxiety, brain damage, headaches, insomnia, hallucinations

THE LUNGS
Marijuana, narcotics, tranquillizers, stimulants, tobacco

Effects
respiratory damage, lung problems, fetal lung problems, cancer

THE HEART
marijuana, mescaline or Peyote, alcohol, tranquillizers, caffeine

Effects
rapid heart beat, slowing of heart rate, heart disease, strokes, blockage of blood vessels

THE LIVER
narcotics, sedatives, inhalants, tranquillizers, alcohol

Effects
liver damage, infection, hepatitis, cirrhosis, swelling

THE DIGESTIVE SYSTEM

Effects

marijuana, PMA, Psilocybin, caffeine, tobacco, alcohol

increased or decreased appetite, abdominal discomfort, vomiting, ulcers, diarrhoea, upset stomach

THE REPRODUCTIVE SYSTEM

Effects

marijuana, LSD, narcotics, sedatives, tranquillizers, stimulants (tobacco, caffeine, alcohol)

complications during pregnancy or childbirth, impotence, spontaneous abortion, miscarriage and stillbirth.

7

Breakfree!
Say No to Smoking

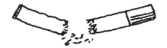

Learning to be a grownup is very exciting. As you grow older, you are able to make more choices about the things you like to do. In order to make choices, however, you need to have the facts and know how your choice will affect you.

Using cigarettes and chewing tobacco is one of those choices. You may see adults smoking or have friends who say it is a "cool" or "super" thing to do. It may even make them look and feel grownup. But the facts are, using tobacco in any form is dangerous to your health. The younger you are when you start smoking, the more it hurts your body. Here are some plain, simple facts:

One cigarette will:

- put carbon monoxide (a deadly gas) into your blood
- cause your heart to start beating faster and harder
- leave a sticky dark substance called tar in your lungs
- make it hard to breath, especially when you're playing.

After several cigarettes, you will:

- begin coughing because the hot gases have burned and irritated your throat
- become weak due to not having enough oxygen in your blood
- have shortness of breath due to shrinking air passages

- get stains on your teeth from tobacco tar
- have bad breath and have less ability to taste food
- get more colds and other illness due to damaged air passages
- smell bad from tobacco smoke in your clothes and hair

After smoking for a long time, you will have a much greater chance of getting the following smoking related illness:

- cancer of the mouth, throat, voice box, lungs and stomach
- heart disease
- stroke, when narrowed blood vessels break in your brain
- emphysema, a fatal condition that exists when lungs have been damaged beyond repair.

7

Smokeless or Chewing Tobacco

Just because you don't light up, tobacco is still deadly. If you chew tobacco, you will get:

- tooth and gum decay, and therefore more visits to the dentist
- discoloured teeth, bad breath, and ugly sores in your mouth
- less ability to taste and smell
- a greater risk of developing mouth cancer.

Don't be fooled into thinking smoking is cool.

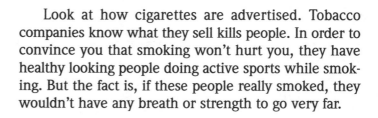

Look at how cigarettes are advertised. Tobacco companies know what they sell kills people. In order to convince you that smoking won't hurt you, they have healthy looking people doing active sports while smoking. But the fact is, if these people really smoked, they wouldn't have any breath or strength to go very far.

Cigarette smoke is just as deadly as smoking itself. Cigarettes contain cyanide, arsenic, formaldehyde, ammonia and nicotine, which is passed on through smoke to non-smokers. Nicotine is a drug. It makes smokers feel relaxed while making their bodies work harder. Smokers begin to crave nicotine and can't stop themselves from smoking more and more. It's a deadly trap you don't want to fall into.

Talk over the facts with your family and how you feel about smoking. If someone in your family smokes, ask them why. Try to work together to find a way to help them cut down on smoking or quit altogether. You will both have healthier, happier lives when you do.

These are the two things I did to develop myself in Cubs that I remember best:

1. _____

2. _____

Some special things I learned were:

_____

_____

Some things I'd like to try next time or when I'm a Scout are:

_____

_____

_____

_____

_____

_____

_____

CHAPTER 8

The Home and Community

Activity Area

Being part of a family means doing your share to help around the home. It's a big job that not all kids can do. When you do your best to make simple home repairs, do chores and learn about safety, you show what a responsible person you are becoming.

Your home also depends on other people in your community. Police and firefighters keep us safe, hospitals take care of us when we are sick, and TV and radio stations tell us the news. Exploring your community will show you how all these services support your home and other families in your neighbourhood.

Blue Star Activities

Learning how to take care of your home and getting around your community are part of becoming a responsible grownup. These activities will get you started on exploring where you live.

To earn the Blue Star, choose and do any five of the A requirements and any four of the B requirements. These activities can be done by yourself, or with your six, pack, family or friends.

A Requirements

CHECK OFF WHEN COMPLETED AND WRITE THE DATE.

_____2010_____ ☑ 1. Accept and carry out a home chore for 1 month, such as washing dishes, cleaning your room or caring for the family pet.

_____ ☐ 2. With an adult, show how to make simple repairs around your home.

_____ ☐ 3. Discuss with your leader some safety rules when home alone and in dealing with strangers.

_____ ☐ 4. Show how to use a home telephone, a public telephone, and a telephone book. Show you know your own home telephone number and can find emergency numbers in a telephone book.

_____ ☐ 5. Send and receive a simple message in Bliss symbols, Braille, American Sign Language, or another form of communication used by some disabled people.

_____2010_____ ☑ 6. Demonstrate basic first aid skills.

_____ ☐ 7. Make use of two community resources such as a library, museum, playground, recreation centre, skating rink, swimming pool, etc., and tell other Cubs how they can use them.

_____ ☐ 8. On a map of your community, point out the location of your home and three other interesting places, such as your school, the library, your place of worship, your Cub meeting hall, etc.

_____ ☐ 9. Describe the highway codes for pedestrians and cyclists and explain why we have these codes.
_____ ☐ 10. Plan and prepare a party for a family, pack, six or other group.

B Requirements

CHECK OFF WHEN COMPLETED AND WRITE THE DATE.

_____ ☐ 1. Visit a national, provincial or local government building such as a courthouse or city hall. Tell about or make a scrapbook of your visit.
_____ ☐ 2. Visit a municipal service such as the police or fire station, water works, sewage treatment plant, etc. Tell about or make a scrapbook of your visit.
_____ ☐ 3. Visit a communications service, such as a newspaper plant, telephone exchange, printing press, radio or T.V. station, etc. Tell about or make a scrapbook of your visit.
_____ ☐ 4. Visit a transportation centre, such as an airport, a railway station, bus depot, taxi dispatcher, etc. Tell about or make a scrapbook of your visit.
_____ ☐ 5. Carry out an accident and fire prevention check of your home, garage, Cub meeting place, or community. With your family, draw an emergency escape plan for your home.
_____ ☐ 6. Make a list or point out in your meeting place and community what services are available for disabled people.

I completed my Blue Star requirements on:

_____
(date)

Badge Activities

If you're ready for more responsibility, here are some more challenging activities. These activities can be done by yourself, or with your six, pack, family or friends.

Disability Awareness Badge

CHECK OFF WHEN COMPLETED AND WRITE THE DATE.

Do any four of the following:

___2010___ ☑ 1. Recognize the International Symbol of Accessibility and point out places where this sign is found.

_____ ☐ 2. Discuss with your leader how building entrances, water fountains, elevators, public telephones and washrooms, and sidewalk corner curbs can be made more accessible to persons in wheelchairs.

___2010___ ☑ 3. Visit your library and find out how books are made available for visually impaired people.

_____ ☐ 4. Meet with a social worker, agency representative or knowledgable adult as to what services are available in your community to people with various disabilities.

_____ ☐ 5. Talk to your gym teacher, Parks and Recreation department or leader about how disabled persons participate and compete in various sports.

_____ ☐ 6. Talk to a representative from the phone company, TV station or other knowledgable adult about what services are available for the hearing impaired.

_____ ☐ 7. Find out what American Sign Language (ASL) is. Learn some sign language and how to sign your name.

_____ ☐ 8. Where possible, meet with a disabled person and talk about that person's personal interests and activities.

I completed my Disability Awareness Badge requirements on:

_____
(date)

Family Helper Badge

CHECK OFF WHEN COMPLETED AND WRITE THE DATE.

With the help of an adult, do any seven of the following:

_____ ☐ 1. Show how to use the kitchen stove or microwave oven safely, and then make tea, coffee, hot chocolate, soup or cook an egg. Show how much quicker a pot with a lid on will boil than a pot without a lid. Explain how this helps you to cook with less energy. Explain how using a microwave to heat up food instead of the stove will help reduce energy use and climate change.

Dec. 2
2011 ☑ 2. Set a table for a two course meal for your family.

☑ 3. Know how to load a dishwasher and when it is full, how to turn it on. Or show the proper way to wash dishes by hand. Explain how only running a dish-washer when it is full will help reduce how much water and energy are used.

X2011 ☑ 4. Clean windows and mop a floor.

Nov. 21 ☑ 5. Make a bed and clean and tidy a room.

Nov. 11 ☑ 6. Vacuum a rug.

_____ ☐ 7. Show the correct way to answer callers at the door and on the telephone, and show how to pass on a message.

2011 ☑ 8. Wash and dry a load of laundry and iron your neckerchief. Explain how hanging clothes to dry will help reduce the amount of energy you use.

_____ ☐ 9. Show how to recycle, compost and dispose of household garbage. See if you can reduce the amount of garbage you are throwing out each week by putting this into action.

_____ ☐ 10. Sew on a badge and a button.

_____ ☐ 11. Discuss how to properly dispose of household toxic waste such as paint, oil, paint thinner, old medicine, cleaners and batteries.

2010

August
2010

☑ 12. Wash an automobile.

☐ 13. Keep an entrance to a home clear of snow for one month.

☐ 14. Water a lawn or garden for one month. Explain what time of day is best to water plants to conserve water.

☐ 15. Show that you can help reduce your familiy's energy costs by turning off lights and electrical equipment that are not being used during a one week period.

I completed my Family Helper Badge requirements on:

2011 *CBPayton*

(date)

CLIMATE CHANGE CHALLENGE
DÉFI CHANGEMENT CLIMATIQUE

(See page 259)

Family Safety Badge

CHECK OFF WHEN COMPLETED AND WRITE THE DATE.

With the help of an adult, complete the following:

_____ ☐ 1. Help reduce the risk of fire and burns in the home by checking that:
    a) Matches and flammable liquids are stored properly and out of reach of small children
    b) Paint, paper and rags are away from heat
    c) Pot handles are turned toward the back of the stove to prevent the pots being knocked or grabbed by small children
    d) Your hot water tank is set below 54°C (130°F) to help prevent scalding

_____ ☐ 2. Show how to test and care for a smoke alarm.

_____ ☐ 3. Help reduce the risk of poisoning in the home by checking that:
    a) Poisons, cleaners and medicines are out of reach of children. Show how to find poison information on household products labelled as poison.
    b) Food containers such as pop bottles are not being used to store poisonous products
    c) Food is stored safely and handled properly

_____ ☐ 4. Know and draw the following hazardous products symbols for poison, flammable, explosive and corrosive. Find some products that are labelled this way.

_____ ☐ 5. Show how to lock and secure all windows, doors and other entry ways into your home.

_____ ☐ 6. Tell or demonstrate what to do if:
    a) The lights go out in your home
    b) A fuse blows or circuit breaker trips
    c) There is a broken water pipe
    d) There is a smell of natural gas
    e) The drains back up

_____ ☐ 7. Help reduce the risk of falls in the home by checking that halls, stairs, and walkways are clear of objects.

8

                ☐ 8. Do one of the following projects:
a) Make a poster or display that show the dangers of playing on or near train tracks, trestles, crossings and/or train yards.
b) Make a poster or display that shows the dangers of touching power lines with a stick or ladder, climbing on electrical power poles, towers and substations, poking electrical outlets and/or pulling toast out of a toaster with a knife or fork.
c) Make a poster or display that shows the dangers of playing around storm sewers, construction sites, garbage dumps or dumpsters, ice covered water or water areas, vacant buildings, farm machinery, quarries, old wells and/or unfriendly animals.

                ☐   9. Make a list of emergency numbers, such as: police, fire, ambulance, etc., and post it by a phone in your home.

I completed my Family Safety Badge requirements on:

_____

(date)

200

First Aider Badge

CHECK OFF WHEN COMPLETED AND WRITE THE DATE.

With the help of an adult, do the following:

_____ ☐ 1. Explain:
a) The meaning of first aid
b) The meaning of medical aid
c) The three most important measures
you must learn to save a life.

_____ ☐ 2. Do the following:
a) Demonstrate rescue breathing.
b) Demonstrate first aid for a severe wound.
c) Show how to care for an unconscious person.
d) Show how to give first aid for a burn or scald.
e) Show how to give first aid for a wound that is
bleeding.
f) Show how to stop a nose bleed.
g) Show what to do if your clothes or another
person's clothes catch fire.
h) Describe the signs of frost-bite and how to treat it.
i) Describe what to do if an insect or animal bites
you or another person.
j) Explain how to prevent and treat hypothermia
and overheating.

Note: Direct human contact (human to human) is not required for Cubs practising rescue breathing.

You can get more information from the local office of St. John Ambulance or The Canadian Red Cross that serves your area.

I completed my First Aider Badge requirements on:

$\underline{\qquad 2010 \qquad}$

(date)

Guide Badge

CHECK OFF WHEN COMPLETED AND WRITE THE DATE.

_____ ☐ 1. Show that you can politely give clear, simple directions to someone asking his or her way. Describe what you would do if a stranger offered you a ride or asked you to come along to show him or her how to get to a place.

_____ ☐ 2. Describe how to call for fire fighters, police or ambulance.

_____ ☐ 3. Show on a map the route of your local bus, or school bus **or** a direct route from your home to the centre of your community.

_____ ☐ 4. Describe how to get to the main highways around your community.

_____ ☐ 5. Describe or point out on a map the location of as many of the following as are found in your community:
a) nearest mail box or post office
b) police station
c) hospital/doctor
d) school
e) drug store
f) public telephone
g) fire station or alarm box
h) railway or bus station
i) gas station
j) hotel or motel
k) block parent

I completed my Guide Badge requirements on:

_____
(date)

Home Repair Badge

CHECK OFF WHEN COMPLETED AND WRITE THE DATE.

With the help of an adult, do any seven of the following:

_____ ☐ 1. Show how to turn on and off the electric power supply and the water supply in your home. Explain how to turn off the gas supply if your home uses gas.

_____ ☐ 2. Replace a light bulb in a socket. With an adult, check in your house which light bulbs could be replaced by energy efficient fluorescent bulbs.

_____ ☐ 3. Replace a tap washer.

_____ ☐ 4. Lubricate a door hinge and/or lock.

_2012_ ☑ 5. Finish a wood surface and stain.

_2012_ ☑ 6. Properly prepare and paint a piece of wood or metal.

_____ ☐ 7. Help keep work areas, such as garage or basement, clean and tidy for one month.

_____ ☐ 8. Resod or reseed a worn out part of a lawn.

_____ ☐ 9. Tell or show how to clear a stopped up sink or toilet.

_____ ☐ 10. Replace a doorknob or install any kind of door or window lock.

I completed my Home Repair Badge requirements on:

_____
(date)

SCOUTS CANADA

CLIMATE CHANGE CHALLENGE
DÉFI CHANGEMENT CLIMATIQUE

(See page 259)

Law Awareness Badge

CHECK OFF WHEN COMPLETED AND WRITE THE DATE.

3/28/12 GRS ☑ 1. Talk to your six about the laws of the Wolf Cub pack and what they mean. What rules should you have in your six so that everyone can enjoy Cubs more? What might happen if your pack or six did not have rules?

_____ ☐ 2. Talk to one of your leaders about who makes the laws in our country and why these laws are important to us. Who is responsible for making sure our laws are followed? Who can you ask for help if you see a law being broken?

_____ ☐ 3. For any four of the following situations, explain to your six what the laws are and why we have them.
   a) Crossing private property
   b) Burning or damaging private property
   c) Traffic laws for bicycles, pedestrians and automobiles
   d) Littering
   e) Hurting other people
   f) Taking what doesn't belong to you
   g) Polluting or damaging the environment
   h) Drinking and driving
   i) Taking illegal drugs

   Talk about what would happen in your neighbourhood if you didn't have these laws.

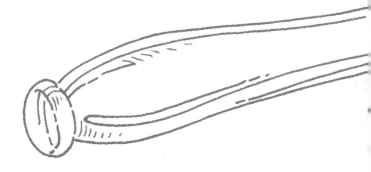

_____ ☐ 4. Talk with your parents or guardian about the following situations and decide what you would do for any four of them.
a) Someone breaks into or damages your house.
b) Someone steals your bicycle.
c) A stranger asks questions about your parents, neighbours, or yourself.
d) You see someone hurting or bullying another person.
e) Someone asks you to break open a school locker.
f) Someone offers you drugs, alcohol, or cigarettes.
g) Someone dares you to shoplift.

I completed my Law Awareness Badge requirements on:

_____
(date)

8

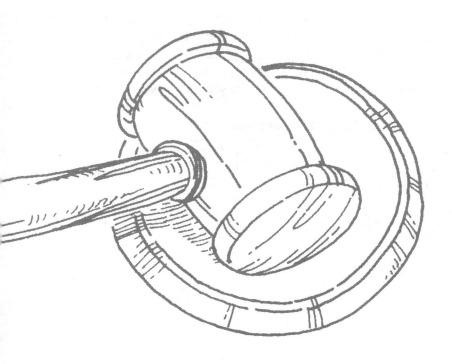

Pet Care Badge

CHECK OFF WHEN COMPLETED AND WRITE THE DATE.

Dec.18 ☑ 1. Keep and take care of a pet for three months or, if this is not possible, help take care of another person's pet for three months.

Dec. 7 2011 ☑ 2. Explain and obey local regulations for keeping an animal as a pet.

Nov. 13 ☑ 3. Read a book about your pet.

Dec. 7 2011 ☑ 4. Explain the care of the pet: shelter, feeding, common illnesses and inoculations, cleanliness, exercise, and training.

Dec. 7 2011 ☑ 5. Describe how to be careful around a strange animal and what to do if you suspect it might have a dangerous disease such as rabies.

Dec. 7 2011 ☑ 6. Explain how and why the pet became domesticated.

Hint: Requirement 6 works for animals like cats, horses, and dogs. For some animals (like snakes), it will be hard to learn when they became domesticated, if they ever did. If, for any reason, you can't care for a pet at home, ask one of your leaders how you can arrange to care for a pet elsewhere. Check the library in your community or at school for books on pets.

I completed my Pet Care Badge requirements on:

Dec. 7 2011
(date)

206

The Canadian Family Care Award

Want a chance to show how grown-up and responsible you really are? Then here is your chance! These activities can be done by yourself, or with your six, pack, family or friends.

CHECK OFF WHEN COMPLETED AND WRITE THE DATE.

To achieve this award, you must complete the following:

_2011_ ☑ 1. Earn the Blue Star.

_2010_ ☑ 2. Earn the following Home and Community related badges:

  a) Family Safety
  b) First Aider
  c) Disability Awareness

_2011_ ☑ 3. Earn one other Home and Community related badge.

_____ ☐ 4. Help show other Cubs how to do a family care skill of your choice.

I completed my Canadian Family Care Award requirements on:

_____
    (date)

This Award may be worn on your Scout sash after you become a Scout.

Staying Safe

At some time, you may come into a situation that is unsafe, or even dangerous. Here are some tips to help you stay safe. Talk over these tips with your parents, or another grown-up you respect.

- Trust your feelings. If a situation or person is making you feel uncomfortable, it's O.K. to say "NO", and leave. Remember it is all right to say "NO" to anyone who wants you to do something you know is wrong.

- Tell your parent or an adult you trust if something happens that bothers you. It's not your fault if something bad happens. You don't have to keep it a secret, no matter what anyone says.

- If it really seems too hard to talk about, write a note. Or call the **Kid's Help Phone** number: 1-800-668-6868. It's a special phone line for children who need help or advice.

Some situations invite danger. Play it smart and avoid them!

- Avoid hanging around lonely parks, woods, parking lots or even school yards late after school.

- Work out the best route to school or other places you go to often. Check the route with a parent for possible unsafe places, and then stick with this route.

- Go places with buddies when possible.

- Say NO if a grown-up invites you alone into his or her home or car, unless your parent has given permission and knows where you are. If a grown-up you don't know asks for directions, step well back before answering. Or just leave.

- Never take gifts or candy from a stranger or anyone else without asking your parents first.

- Never open the door when you are home alone.

- Never say you're home alone if you answer the phone. Tell whoever is calling that your parents can't come to the phone and to call back later or leave a message.

Sometimes you may need the help of other adults. Talk to your parents or another adult you trust about how to handle these situations. Here are some ideas:

- You choose the person you want to help you. People to choose to ask for help are:

    - ❏ Police officers and Firefighters
    - ❏ Block Parents
    - ❏ Mothers or Fathers with children
    - ❏ Uniformed bus or subway drivers
    - ❏ Teachers
    - ❏ People who work in stores.

- Tell the grown-up you choose what has happened and ask them to phone your parents, or to wait with you until they arrive.

- If you happen to find a needle (the kind doctors use to give people injections), pills, or something you think is not safe, don't touch it. Go tell your parents, teacher, or a police officer what you have found and where.

- If someone tries to force you to go with them, here is a way to protect yourself:

    - Scream, "Help! Kidnapper!" and scatter your belongings. Keep screaming.
    - Fall to the ground, spin, and kick. Keep kicking until help comes or you can run away.

Disability Awareness

If you are like most people, you can run and jump, hear and see, and think clearly. Some people however, cannot do these things as well as most of us. This situation is called having a disability.

A caring community looks after the needs of all kinds of people. Look around when you are out. You'll notice special parking spots near store doors for people who have a hard time walking. Street level sidewalk corners and ramps allow people in wheel chairs to get up on sidewalks and into buildings. Special receivers and computers help people who can't see or hear to be able to use the telephone. Check out your community and write down the ways your community helps disabled people.

My community helps disabled people by having:

_____

_____

_____

Using a Public Telephone

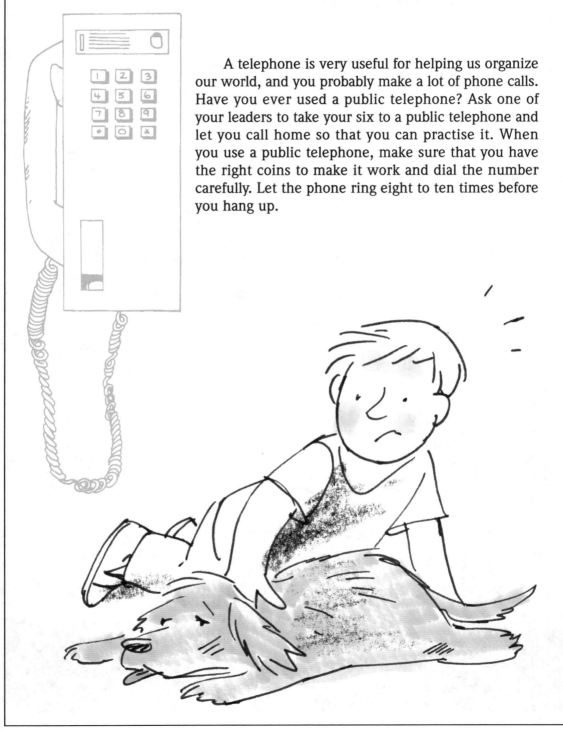

A telephone is very useful for helping us organize our world, and you probably make a lot of phone calls. Have you ever used a public telephone? Ask one of your leaders to take your six to a public telephone and let you call home so that you can practise it. When you use a public telephone, make sure that you have the right coins to make it work and dial the number carefully. Let the phone ring eight to ten times before you hang up.

In most provinces, you can dial "O" without paying any money if there is an emergency. Tell the operator what the problem is and ask to be connected with the proper emergency number. In some provinces, you may have to use a coin to call the operator, but you'll likely get it back when you are finished the call.

You can even dial "O" and ask the operator to connect you with your home if you need help from your parents and don't have money. But because your family will be charged extra on its phone bill, you should not do this if you don't have to.

Some areas have 911 as a special emergency number you can dial without paying money. Ask an adult to find out whether your area has 911, but only use this number if there is an emergency.

The public telephone I used is at:

_____.

(location)

The number I called was _____ *and the*

person I talked to was _____.

(name)

It cost me _____ *to make the call.*

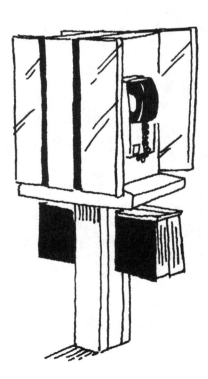

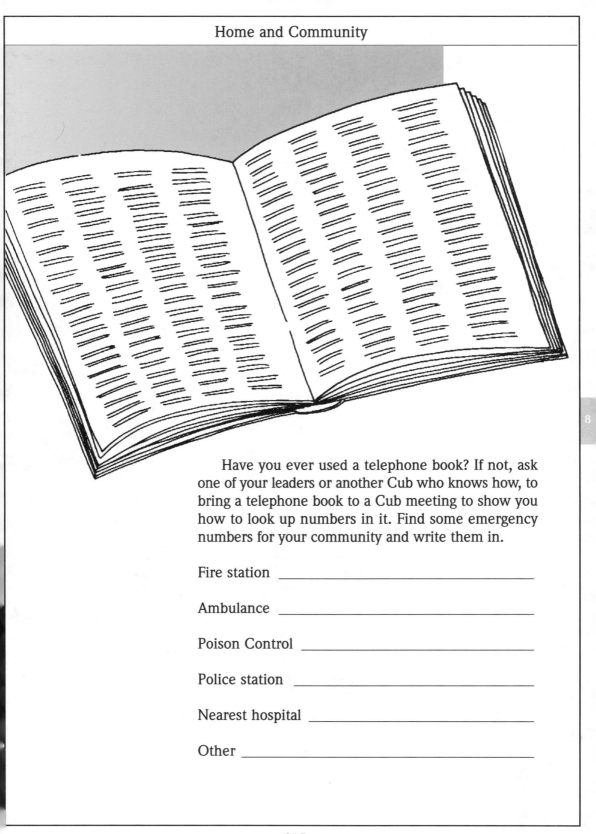

Have you ever used a telephone book? If not, ask one of your leaders or another Cub who knows how, to bring a telephone book to a Cub meeting to show you how to look up numbers in it. Find some emergency numbers for your community and write them in.

Fire station _____

Ambulance _____

Poison Control _____

Police station _____

Nearest hospital _____

Other _____

First Aid

One good way to keep our world well organized is to help each other when we have problems. You can help in a very special way if you learn how to give first aid. First aid is quick help to ease an injured person before he or she can get to a doctor. Here are some important things you can do to give first aid to an injured person.

1. Get help. This part is the most important! If there is an accident, get a doctor, nurse, leader, or other adult as quickly as you can. If at all possible, stay with the injured person and send someone else for help.

2. Check to see if the injured person is breathing. If not, open an airway and perform rescue breathing.

3. Stop bleeding. If blood is pumping out of a wound, it can be very dangerous. Press hard and keep on pressing or quickly tie a bandage or cloth tightly around the wound. Keep pressing until the bleeding stops. If there is a piece of glass or metal deep in the wound, do not take it out because that could cause more damage. Just press hard as close as possible around the wound. Lay the person down. If the wound is on an arm or a leg, try to lift up the arm or leg and keep pressing at the same time to help slow the bleeding. Send for a doctor or another adult.

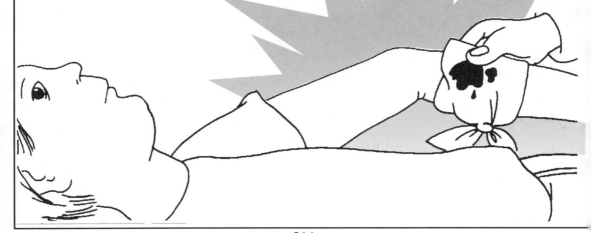

4. Control shock. Lay the person on their stomach, with their head turned to the side and cover with a blanket or coat. Don't move them though, if you think they might have hurt their neck or back.

5. Fracture (broken bones). If you think a bone is broken, do not move the injured person. Send for adult help.

6. Burn or scald. A burn is caused by flame or something hot like a stove. A scald is caused by hot water or steam. To ease the pain and keep the burn from spreading, treat burns and scalds with cold water. For serious burns where the skin is broken or blistered, send for help immediately. For less serious burns where the skin is just red, put the burned part in cold water and keep it clean. NEVER remove burned clothing, even if it is stuck to the skin. NEVER break any blisters. NEVER put on creams or lotions or grease. Send for help.

7. Animal Bite. Stay away from the animal because it might bite you. Tell an adult what kind of animal made the bite and point it out if you can do so safely. Get the injured person to a doctor.

8. Something in the eye. Do not let the person rub the eye. Cover both eyes with clean material and get the person to a doctor. It is important to cover both eyes because, if someone can see with one eye, he or she moves the eyeball. That causes the other eyeball to move and scrape against whatever is in it. And that can cause more injury.

9. Cuts and Scrapes. Wash with plain soap and water. If there is dirt in the wound, wash it out under running tap water (don't use water on bleeding wounds). If you must cover it, use the cleanest material possible.

10. Bruises. Hold the bruise in very cold water or place a cold wet towel or piece of ice on it. This often will ease the pain and may reduce the swelling.

11. Nose Bleed. Pinch the nostrils with head slightly forward. If bleeding doesn't stop in 10 minutes, see a doctor.

12. Insect Sting. Look for a stinger in the skin, swelling or difficulty in breathing. If you spot any of these, get adult help quickly.

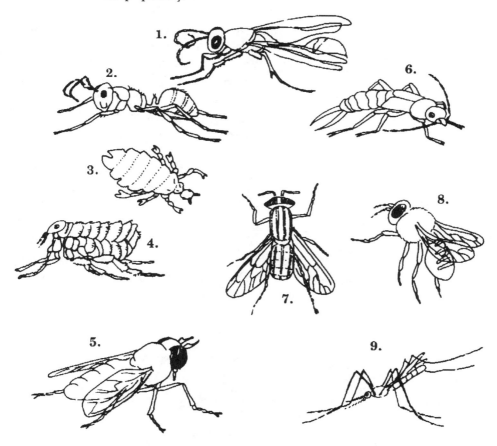

These insects bite or sting. Can you identify them?

1. Mud wasp, 2. black carpenter ant, 3. head louse, 4. flea, 5. horse fly, 6. earwig, 7. deerfly, 8. honey bee, 9. mosquito.

13. Heat Exhaustion. Caused by not drinking enough fluids while active in hot weather. Someone with heat exhaustion will have a pale face, clammy skin and feel tired or sick to their stomach. Lay the person down in the shade with their feet higher than their head. Give sips of cool water, but ONLY if the person is conscious. Let the person rest and continue to drink until they feel better. Get adult help.

14. Heatstroke. You can tell that someone has heatstroke if the person's face and body is hot and red. The person may act confused, become dizzy and pass out. Move them to a shady area. Check for breathing, then start cooling by bathing or applying wet cloths to their head and body. Continue to cool the person until their temperature becomes normal. Give sips of cool water, but ONLY if the person is conscious. Get a doctor quickly.

15. Hypothermia. This condition happens when your body gets too cold to warm up on its own. It is a very serious condition that you can see because the person shivers uncontrollably and may have numb hands and feet. Put the person in a warm dry place, give them a warm drink, and get adult help right away. Know how to stay warm to keep it from happening to you.

16. Frost-bite. This happens when part of your skin surface is frozen. Often the skin will turn white. The face, toes and fingers are the easiest places to get frost-bite. Warm a frostbitten area slowly with the palms of your hand or under your armpit. NEVER rub, put snow on the area, or warm the part too fast. Always get adult help.

17. Medical Alert. Know how to check for and what to do about a medical alert bracelet worn by an injured person.

18. Emergencies. Know how to find the poison control and other emergency telephone numbers for your area.

First aid is a serious business. If you want to learn it at all, you must learn it well and practise it regularly so that you won't forget it and make a mistake. If you learn it well, some day you may save someone a lot of pain and suffering. You may even save someone's life.

Practising first aid can be fun. Ask Akela or another leader to help you and some of the other Cubs practise it. Maybe a parent of one of the Cubs in your pack is a doctor or nurse who will come to a meeting to help you learn. Try to get some red poster paint or actor's makeup and paint gruesome wounds on yourselves, then practise treating those wounds. Perhaps, when you are good at first aid, you and the others can do a skit that shows one or two Cubs having an accident and the others treating them and getting help. See what you can dream up to put on for the rest of the pack.

The St. John Ambulance of Canada has a fun activity booklet called *"We Can Help"* that tells a lot about first aid. Ask Akela or an adult friend to help you get a copy.

This is what I did at a meeting where we practised first aid:

_____

_____

_____

_____

This is what we looked like when we practised.

Do you know where most accidents happen? At home! That means the best way to start protecting yourself and your family is to do a safety check of your home. Here's how to do it.

Make a Fire Escape Plan

1. Draw a big picture of every room of your home on each floor, something like this.

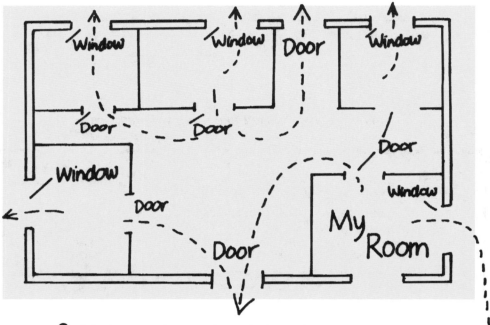

2. Mark every door and window on the picture.

3. For every room on every floor, draw a line showing the quickest escape route to the outside in case of fire. Draw another route you can use if the first route is blocked.

4. Show your picture to your parents and ask them to hold a fire drill to help your whole family learn the best way to escape.

Home Safety Check

      With your parents, look carefully at every room in your house, including the garage if there is one.

Check for anything that might be dangerous, such as:
- a) old rags, newspapers, or liquids that might burn
- b) smoke detectors that don't work (dead batteries)
- c) loose or frayed electrical wires that might cause a spark
- d) poisons stored within reach of children
- e) loose rugs that might slip
- f) guns that aren't locked up
- g) matches left lying around
- h) electrical fuses that are too big for the circuit
- i) toys and other things left where people might trip on them

8

Household Hazardous Wastes Identification

Poison

Materials that are poisonous or lethal to you, your family and pets, even in small quantities

Flammable

Liquids that can ignite

Explosive

Materials that can create an explosion or produce deadly vapours

Corrosive

Substances that eat and wear away at many materials

Radioactive

Materials that give off small doses of radiation (e.g. ionizing smoke detectors)

Make a list of everything you find that might be dangerous and ask your parents to let you help get rid of all hazards.

These are the dangerous things I found in my house:

_____

_____

_____

When you've finished your home safety check, show your work to one of your leaders. Talk to your six about what you found and did. Suggest that your six do a safety check of the building where the pack meets.

Look for the same things that you looked for in your home safety check. Try to find as many ways as possible to escape from your hall in case of fire. Maybe Akela can hold a fire drill for your pack so that you can test the escape routes.

Here's a map of our meeting hall with emergency exits and alarms.

After you've checked your home and Cub hall, you can check your community for safety. Ask Akela to let one of the leaders take your six through your neighbourhood. Look for things like:

1. Locations of fire alarms
2. Places where crossing the street is dangerous
3. Things such as construction sites, dumps, or storm sewers where children could be trapped
4. Power boxes and stations, and railroad tracks.

Because every neighbourhood is different, you will need to use your eyes and imagination to figure out what might be dangerous.

These are the dangerous things my pack or six found on our community safety check:

Dangers   What We Did About It

1. _____ _____

2. _____ _____

3. _____ _____

A Scrapbook of Visits

Does your pack go places? Ask Akela to take the pack on visits to places around your home and community.

A fire station is always exciting, and you can learn how to protect yourself against fire, too.

Maybe you can visit the council chambers of your village, city, or town, or a local Scout Area meeting. If you do, ask your guide if you can sit in the mayor or reeve's chair for a minute. Then you can imagine what laws you might pass if you were in charge: free ice cream bars for Cubs every Friday; a school holiday every Monday!

If you live near an airport, you might get a chance to go up into the control tower to hear the pilots talking on the radio.

It can be fun to keep a scrapbook of your trips. There are so many places you can go — a farm, zoo, bottle factory, tree nursery, library, city hall, fire station, T.V. station, weather station, shipyard, airport, mine. You can probably think of a lot more to add to the list.

What was the most interesting thing you saw on your visit? Draw a picture of it. What was the least interesting thing? Draw a picture of it, too. Did you collect any post cards or folders? Tape or glue them into your scrapbook. Did you learn any safety tips? Write them down in your book.

After each visit you make, show your scrapbook to your six.

Here's a list of some of the more interesting visits I made as a Cub:

_____

_____

_____

_____

_____

_____

Put a photo here of the most interesting place you visited.

*These were the two things I did around my home
and community that I enjoyed a lot:*

1. _____

_____

2. _____

_____

*These are some of the special things I learned about
how and why communities take care of people:*

*These are some of the things I'd like to do next
time or when I'm in Scouts:*

_____

_____

_____

_____

_____

CHAPTER 9

Canada and the World

Activity Area

What do you think of when someone says the word "CANADA"? Do you see hockey, fishing or hiking in the woods? Can you smell fried clams, hotdogs, fresh strawberry jelly or baked salmon? Do you remember when the leaves turned colour, the big snowstorms, the tulips first bloom or that hot, sandy day at the beach? Canada is all this and so much more. We live in one of the largest, most plentiful countries in the world. Our greatest natural resource, however, is not our oceans, forests or farmlands, but our people. Every day Canada shows how people from different backgrounds and beliefs can come together to live and work together in peace.

Our commitment to peace and hard work is well known throughout the world. When the Canadian flag flies high in another country, local people recognize us as people who can be trusted and depended upon. Canada plays a growing role in international trade, communications, medicine, and the arts. It is an exciting time to be a Cub in Canada. The world and beyond is becoming like one big backyard!

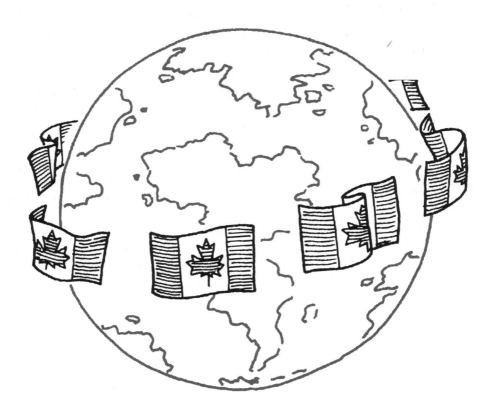

9

Purple Star Activities

Canada and the world is a big place to learn about. Here's a good place to start you on your way.

To earn the Purple Star, choose and do any six of the A requirements and a minimum of five of the B requirements. These activities can be done by yourself, or with your six, pack, family or friends.

A Requirements

CHECK OFF WHEN COMPLETED AND WRITE THE DATE.

Oct.17 ☑ 1. Give the history and draw a picture of the Canadian flag. Also draw the flags of two other countries.

Oct. 17 ☑ 2. Recite or sing "O Canada", our national anthem.

_____ ☐ 3. Draw or trace a map of Canada and include such features as provincial and territorial boundaries, capital cities, your home location, occupations common to the various regions and natural features.

_____ ☐ 4. Make a simple scrapbook describing the life of one or more important Canadians of your choice.

_____ ☐ 5. Discuss with your leader the benefits you and your community receive from doing community service projects.

_____ ☐ 6. Discuss with an adult what some of our Rights and Freedoms are as Canadians. Also discuss what freedom and prejudice mean to you.

_____ ☐ 7. Make a chart of your pack or six and see how many cultures are represented.

_____ ☐ 8. Participate in an activity which explores the traditions of your own faith.

_____ ☐ 9. Participate in an activity which explores the traditions of a religion other than your own.

_____ ☐ 10. Participate in an activity where you explore the traditions of a culture or country other than your own.

_____ ☐ 11. Look through a catalogue, newspaper or magazine for products which are made in another country and sold in Canada. Find products made in Canada that are sold in other countries.

_____ ☐ 12. Make a presentation describing Canadian space technology and travel.

9

B Requirements

CHECK OFF WHEN COMPLETED AND WRITE THE DATE.

_____ ☐ 1. Participate in a local food bank drive.

_____ ☐ 2. Participate in a project to collect items for the needy, such as clothes or toys.

_____ ☐ 3. Assist a Service Agency in a service project. (eg. Red Cross, Cystic Fibrosis Foundation, etc.)

_____ ☐ 4. Participate in providing service for your place of worship.

_____ ☐ 5. Participate in any environmental cleanup or beautification project.

_____ ☐ 6. Participate in an Adopt-a-Friend project for a special person, group, community or environment.

_____ ☐ 7. Participate in providing service to your Sponsor or assist your Sponsor in any community service project.

_____ ☐ 8. Make a gift and donate it to a worthy cause.

_____ ☐ 9. Participate in any project which improves access for or awareness of the disabled.

_____ ☐ 10. Participate in providing service to your school.

_____ ☐ 11. Assist a Colony as a Keeo for three months.

_____ ☐ 12. Participate in a project that supports the Canadian Scout Brotherhood Fund or Community Development Projects.

_____ ☐ 13. Participate in a community service project not listed above.

_____ ☐ 14. Learn about one of Canada's peacekeeping missions. Talk to a veteran or soldier who has served on Canada's behalf in a conflict or peacekeeping mission.

I completed my Purple Star requirements on:

_____2010_____
(date)

Badge Activities

Are you ready to learn more about Canada and the role Canadians play in the world? Then try some of these fun and challenging activities. These activities can be done by yourself, or with your six, pack, family or friends.

Aboriginal Awareness Badge

CHECK OFF WHEN COMPLETED AND WRITE THE DATE.

Do any four of the following requirements:

☐ 1. Tell about or show four or more items that were invented by Aboriginal people and which we still use today.

☐ 2. Make a list of Aboriginal words that are used as names of places, such as provinces and territories, cities, towns, parks, roads and waterways. Discover the Aboriginal meaning of these words.

☐ 3. Learn about some of the Aboriginal people who first lived in your area. Using historical information and designs, make a model or display that shows their dwellings, how they travelled, their writing and art forms, and objects used for daily living.

☐ 4. Learn an Aboriginal game, song, dance or story and share it with your six or pack.

☐ 5. Tell how an Aboriginal people's way of life is affected by the part of the country in which they live.

☐ 6. Discover and tell how Aboriginal people helped early explorers and pioneers to settle in Canada.

☐ 7. If possible, arrange to visit with an Aboriginal person. Find out how that person's life is similar to or different from how Aboriginal people lived long ago.

I completed my Aboriginal Awareness Badge requirements on:

20 10 / 20 1

(date)

Canadian Heritage Badge

CHECK OFF WHEN COMPLETED AND WRITE THE DATE.

Do any seven of the following requirements:

_____ ☐ 1. Learn a Canadian folksong and its origins, and then sing it with your six or pack.

__2010__ ☑ 2. Make a scrapbook about a famous Canadian, telling when he or she lived, and what their accomplishments were.

_____ ☐ 3. Learn a Canadian legend or folktale. Tell it to your six or pack.

_____ ☐ 4. Do EITHER (a) or (b):

    a) Visit another part of Canada and make a collection of things that you see there. Present your collection to your six or pack.

    b) Make a presentation about a city in Canada other than where you live. How big is it? When was it founded? What is it famous for? What is Canada like near that city? (Hint: Write to the Chamber of Commerce or Tourism Board to get answers.)

_____ ☐ 5. Visit a local museum. Draw a picture of some of the exhibits or things you see. Show your pictures to your six or pack, and tell them what you liked about the museum and what you learned from visiting it.

_____ ☐ 6. Tell your six or pack about a cultural group in Canada. What are their traditions? What languages does the group speak? How has this group contributed to Canada's culture?

_____ ☐ 7. Make a presentation about Aboriginal people in Canada. Meet with an Aboriginal person if possible, to learn more about the history, traditions and contributions of local Aboriginal people.

_____ ☐ 8. Contact a Cub in another part of Canada. Ask the Cub what Canada is like there, and what the people like to do.

__2012__ ☑ 9. Draw or trace a simple map of Canada, showing the provinces and territories, capital cities, and other main features you can discover.

_____ ☐ 10. Learn the Wolf Cub Promise, Law and Grand Howl in another language of your choice.

_____ ☐ 11. Learn about one of Canada's peacekeeping missions. Talk to a veteran or soldier who has served on Canada's behalf in a conflict or peacekeeping mission.

I completed my Canadian Heritage Badge requirements on:

_____

(date)

International Trade Badge

CHECK OFF WHEN COMPLETED AND WRITE THE DATE.

Do any five of the following requirements.

_____ ☐ 1. Make a list of at least eight items around your home (i.e. groceries, clothes, electronics, etc.) that were grown or produced outside Canada. What countries did they come from? Locate these countries on a map and then find out how the items got to Canada.

_____ ☐ 2. Pick any five spices (i.e. cinnamon, nutmeg, clove, pepper, turmeric). Where did they come from? Find out their history and how they first arrived in other parts of the world.

_____ ☐ 3. Identify at least two different gemstones. Where did they come from? Find out how they have been traded through history.

_____ ☐ 4. Find a business in your area that exports or imports products to or from other countries. Find out where these products have come from, and/or where they are going and how they were transported.

_____ ☐ 5. Find out how airplanes carry both cargo and passengers at the same time. Explain why there are special rules for shipping dangerous goods on airplanes.

_____ ☐ 6. Identify four different types of cargo ships and what each has been specially designed to carry.

_____ ☐ 7. List six things that Canada produces or grows that other countries may want. In return, what things might these other countries trade with us because we don't produce or grow them?

_____ ☐ 8. Learn about the currencies of at least two other countries (i.e. Malaysian ringgits, Chinese yuan, Russian rubles) and compare their value to Canadian currency.

_____ ☐ 9. Many famous explorers went on their voyages looking for new trade routes and new lands. Learn the story of one explorer. Share with your six or leader what the explorer went looking for and what they discovered.

I completed my International Trade Badge requirements on:

_____

(date)

Space Exploration Badge

CHECK OFF WHEN COMPLETED AND WRITE THE DATE.

Do any four of the following requirements:

_____ ☐ 1. Discuss the importance of space technology in Canadian living. This could include:
   a) weather forecasts
   b) communications
   c) search and rescue operations
   d) map making
   e) promoting international cooperation between Canada and other countries.

_____ ☐ 2. Make a drawing or model of a satellite, such as Canada's first satellites Alouette I and II, ISIS or Hermes, or another satellite of your choice.

_____ ☐ 3. Make a presentation about the Space Shuttle, including the Canadarm.

_____ ☐ 4. Design and build a space station. Include living requirements, such as water, air and food supplies, power sources, communications and describe what peaceful activities the space station can be used for.

_____ ☐ 5. Draw or make a model of a rocket, or of a space craft of your own design. Tell about any special features you have included in your model.

_____ ☐ 6. Draw or make a space suit currently in use or one of your own design. Tell about any special features you have included in your model.

_____ ☐ 7. Make a report on or a scrapbook about an astronaut, mission team or space mission of your choice.

I completed my Space Exploration Badge requirements on:

_____
   (date)

World Religions Badge

CHECK OFF WHEN COMPLETED AND WRITE THE DATE.

With your parent's or guardian's permission and assistance from your leader, complete the following requirements.

_____ ☐ 1. Do EITHER (a) or (b):
   a) Visit a place of worship other than your own faith and find out some information about its structure, its contents and the form of worship conducted there.
   b) Meet with a knowledgeable adult who belongs to a denomination or religion other than your own and discover how that person puts their faith into practice in daily life.

_____ ☐ 2. Find out about a religion other than your own and tell your leader about any of its sacred books, holy places, religious customs and special festivals or holidays.

_____ ☐ 3. Discuss with your leader what values many of the world's religions have in common.

I completed my World Religions Badge requirements on:

_2011_
       (date)

World Cubbing Badge

CHECK OFF WHEN COMPLETED AND WRITE THE DATE.

_____ ☐ 1. Find out how Scouts Canada helps developing countries to improve their living conditions. (Ask a leader about the Canadian Scout Brotherhood Fund's Community Development Program and Scoutrees For Canada, or contact your local Scout office.)

_____ ☐ 2. Make a simple scrapbook of another country, containing pictures, drawings or samples of some of the following:
   a) the country's flag
   b) people's daily dress
   c) the country's coins and stamps
   d) interesting places in the country
   e) how people get around
   f) people's houses
   g) what the weather is like
   h) what kind of food people grow and eat
   i) the kinds of things children your age like to do.

——————————— ☐ 3. Do EITHER (a) or (b):

a) Make a presentation to your pack or six on the country you've chosen. Use your scrapbook and talk about:
   - the language or languages people speak
   - the religions people follow
   - the geography and climate
   - the main cities in the country
   - the size of the country
   - the main things people grow and make
   - the kinds of things people do at home, school, work, in their places of worship, and in the outdoors

b) Learn where the people in your neighbourhood or their ancestors came from. Make a presentation for your pack or six on one of these countries, describing:
   - how people in that country express themselves today (language, beliefs, clothing, religion, ceremonies, etc.)
   - why some people from the country came to Canada
   - some of the country's customs your neighbours have kept (eg. religion, food, clothing, games, etc.)

I completed my World Cubbing Badge requirements on:

——————————————————

(date)

245

JE PARLE FRANÇAIS

PARLO ITALIANO

Language Strip

Purpose: Demonstrate an ability to speak in another language.

Requirements:

1. Show you know a language other than your own by conversing on a subject of your choice for 5 minutes.
2. The person to whom you are talking or reporting to must agree that your pronunciation and grammar are basically correct and age appropriate.

You wear the Language Strip on the flap of the left breast pocket of the Cub shirt (see page 35). There are Language Strips available for many languages, including sign language and braille. Ask one of your leaders about them.

Religion in Life Emblem

If the requirements for the Religion in Life Emblem have been set by your religious organization, ask your spiritual advisor or leader to help you earn this award.

The World Citizen Award

Are you interested in what goes on in the world? You'll find these activities both challenging and interesting to do. These activities can be done by yourself, or with your six, pack, family or friends.

CHECK OFF WHEN COMPLETED AND WRITE THE DATE.

To achieve this award you must complete the following:

_____2010_____ ☑ 1. Earn the Purple Star.

_____ ☐ 2. Earn a total of three of the Canada and the World related badges as follows:
   a) The World Religions Badge or the Religion in Life Emblem.
   b) The Aboriginal Awareness Badge or the Canadian Heritage Badge.
   c) One other badge of your choice excluding the Language Strip.

_____ ☐ 3. Choose a current affairs topic of your choice and follow it in the news for at least one week. Report on what had happened and how people were involved.

_____ ☐ 4. Participate in a pack meeting which highlights Canada's role in the United Nations, such as an U.N. night.

I completed my World Citizen Award requirements on:

_____

(date)

This Award may be worn on your Scout sash after you become a Scout.

Our Country and Our Flag

If someone asked you to draw a picture of something that means "Canada", what would you choose? You might draw a map of Canada, a Royal Canadian Mounted Police officer, or even a beaver or hockey player. The easiest thing of all to draw is the Canadian flag. Try it.

Make the flag twice as long as it is high. Divide it into three parts, making the middle part a square. Leave the middle part white and draw a red maple leaf in it. Colour the other two parts red.

When you've drawn your Canadian flag, show it to Akela, your six, your leaders and your pack.

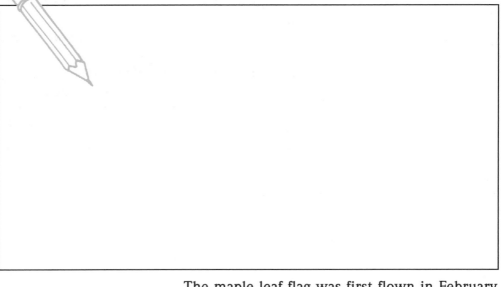

The maple leaf flag was first flown in February 1965. It's a beautiful flag, and many people like to fly it in front of their homes or offices. In some cities and towns, it seems that every building has a flag. Sometime when you see a lot of flags, try to count them to find out how many there are in one place.

You may get a chance to carry the Canadian flag or the Wolf Cub flag in a parade some day. If you do, treat the flag with care and respect and listen carefully to the person who tells you how to carry it.

See if you can find a map of Canada's territory. Try the library, or a travel agency. In the space below, draw a map of Canada, and show where you live. Your leaders, parents and teachers will likely be able to help you.

Our National Anthem

Many times in our lives, we will be asked to sing our national anthem, "O Canada". It is our country's song and tells about the things we believe in. Get to know these words by heart and, when you sing the song, be proud to sing it loud and clear.

O Canada

O Canada! Our home and native land!
True patriot love, in all thy sons command.
With glowing hearts, we see thee rise
The True North strong and free!
From far and wide, O Canada,
We stand on guard for thee.
God keep our land, glorious and free!
O Canada, we stand on guard for thee.
O Canada, we stand on guard for thee.

O Canada

O Canada! Terre de nos aïeux,
Ton front est ceint de fleurons glorieux!
Car ton bras sait porter l'épée,
Il sait porter la croix!
Ton histoire est une épopée
Des plus brillants exploits.
Et ta valeur, de foi trempée,
Protégera nos foyers et nos droits,
Protégera nos foyers et nos droits.

The Royal Anthem

Because, as Canadians, we are asked to do our duty to the Queen, there will be certain times when you will be asked to sing the Royal Anthem. Ask one of your leaders for the tune and see if you can learn these words by heart.

God Save The Queen

God save our gracious Queen,
Long live our noble Queen,
God save the Queen.
Send her victorious,
Happy and glorious,
Long to reign over us;
God save the Queen.

Our Rights as Canadians

Canada is a free country. By that we mean that as people, we are able to think, speak and act - as we please within the law. Not every country is free. In some places, the government decides what people will see, hear, do for a job, or even how to raise a family.

In Canada, our rights are protected by the Charter of Rights and Freedoms. Discuss some of the following rights and freedoms with your family or leaders and what they mean to you. All Canadians have:

- freedom of conscience and religion
- freedom of thought, belief, opinion and expression
- freedom of the press and other media of communications
- freedom of peaceful assembly
- freedom of association
- the right to vote
- the right to enter, remain in and leave Canada
- the right to life, liberty and security of person
- the right of equality before and under the law
- the right of language, education and culture.

Canada's Aboriginal People

Aboriginal people, also known as native people or First Nations, lived in this country long before it was known as Canada. They developed many different languages, customs and cultures, each reflecting their relationship to the land and living things.

Aboriginal people have given Canadian culture a unique quality in that our heritage is not all European based. The canoe, kayak, dog sled, snowshoes and lacrosse were Aboriginal inventions. Aboriginal people were also the first people to grow corn, potatoes, squash, pumpkins and other North American crops. In fact, we owe our country's name to Aboriginal language. The word "Canada" is Laurentian Iroquois for "village".

Ask your family or leaders to help you find other contributions Aboriginal people have made or are making to the area in which you live. You can also make a map of Canada and show where different Aboriginal people live and what languages they speak in those areas.

9

CHAPTER 10

Wolf Cub Specialty Badges

'Of Special Interest'

he Individual Specialty Badge and the Pack Specialty Badge allow individual Cubs and/or an entire pack to design requirements for special interest areas not already covered in the current badge and star system.

Cub Individual Specialty Badge

Purpose: To provide a way to recognize a Cub who has a special interest.

Requirements:

_____ ☐ 1. A Cub may propose a subject and requirements for this badge, or may develop them in cooperation with other members of the pack, the leaders and/or parents. The requirements should be presented to the Sixers' Council and leaders for review.

_____ ☐ 2. Topics selected for this badge should not be covered by any other badges or stars.

_____ ☐ 3. A Cub may hold only one Individual Specialty Badge at a time.

_____ ☐ 4. A Cub may choose a new Individual Specialty once a year.

Note to leaders: Make sure the requirements challenge the Cub's abilities. Remember that the purpose of the badge is to recognize the best effort of the Cub.

I completed my Individual Specialty Badge requirements on:

_____
(date)

Pack Specialty Badge

Purpose: To provide a way to recognize a pack that has a special interest.

Requirements:

_____ ☐ 1. The pack will identify all requirements for this badge with the guidance of leaders.
_____ ☐ 2. A pack may have only one Specialty Badge at a time.
_____ ☐ 3. A pack may change its Specialty Badge once a year if it wishes.

Note to leaders: Make sure the requirements challenge the abilities of those in the pack. Use the creativity of your Sixers' Council to come up with ideas for your Pack Specialty Badge.

I completed my Pack Specialty Badge requirements on:

_____
(date)

10

SCOUTS CANADA

CLIMATE CHANGE CHALLENGE
DÉFI CHANGEMENT CLIMATIQUE

CHAPTER 11

Climate Change Challenge

Crest Requirements

Climate Change Challenge Crest Requirements

To earn the Climate Change Challenge Crest, complete three of the following five badges and do the energy sleuth game and online calculator (found at www.scouts.ca).

Badges: Recycling Badge, World Conservation Badge, Home Repair Badge, Cyclist Badge, Family Helper.

NOTE: The Climate Change Challenge Crest is NOT worn on any uniform or on the sash.

What is Climate Change?

The atmosphere is made up of a layer of gases that surround the Earth. These gases help keep some of the sun's heat in, just like a window in a greenhouse traps heat inside. They help make our planet warm enough to live on.

One of the most common of these gases is called carbon dioxide or "CO_2". It is important for the health of our planet. Did you know that human beings breathe out CO_2 each time we exhale? Plants and trees take in CO_2 through photosynthesis. We also create CO_2 when we use certain fuels, such as coal and oil, to heat our homes and drive our cars.

When we use these fuels we add more and more CO_2 into the atmosphere. A problem starts when too much CO_2 collects in the atmosphere. These gases could raise the temperatures on earth and change our weather patterns. This is what people are calling "climate change". Climate change could bring more forest fires, droughts or floods as well.

How You Can Help Reduce Climate Change at Home

It is important that everyone helps to reduce climate change. There are many ways you can help. You can plant trees with your Cub pack. Trees help to reduce climate change by absorbing CO_2 so it doesn't stay in the atmosphere. You also can help save energy at home – try some of these things that save energy and help to reduce climate change:

Saving Electricity
☐ I turn the lights off when they are not being used
☐ I turn off equipment, like the computer, when it was not being used
☐ I encourage my family to turn off the appliances and equipment when they are not in use.

Saving Hot Water
☐ I turn off the tap when I am not using the water
☐ I take a shower instead of a bath.

Using Less Heat
☐ The temperature of our house is 22 degrees Celsius (or less) in the winter and 22 degrees or more in the summer

☐ I encourage my family to wear slippers and sweaters in the winter to stay warm instead of turning up the thermostat.

Use Less Gasoline
☐ I walk, bike or inline skate for 10 minutes to a destination close to my house (corner store, friend's house, school, club meeting, etc.) two times in one month instead of being driven.

CHAPTER 12

Helping Other Cubs

Yes! You Can!

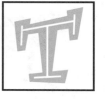he most important part of being in a pack is learning to work as a team. When you help other Cubs, and when they help you, the pack runs more smoothly and everyone has more fun. Here are some ways you can help other Cubs and your leaders.

1. Set an example of how to behave for other Cubs. If they see you listening to your leaders and doing your best in all the activities, they'll want to do the same.
2. Tell Akela what you and the other Cubs like to do. He or she is always looking for exciting pack activities and will be glad to listen to your ideas.
3. Help other Cubs with activities. For example, if the pack is doing a craft and you are finished, offer to help those who may be having problems with theirs.
4. You may be bigger and stronger than many Cubs. When you're playing a game, try not to use your size to knock other Cubs around. Play fair so that everyone has more fun.
5. Sometimes Cubs get into arguments over rules or how something should be done. If you need to find a way to stop arguing, you can use this simple method called ALS. It stands for:

    A - Agree with the person to solve the problem.
    L - Listen to what each person has to say and how each feels.
    S - Summarize the problem and agree on a solution.

Here's how to use ALS:

Step 1 - Agree to solve the problem. The ground rules are:
- No interrupting when the other person talks.
- No name calling or put downs.
- Be honest and tell the truth.

Step 2 - Cub #1 describes what happened and how he or she feels.
Cub #2 repeats what Cub #1 said.
Cub #2 describes what happened and how he or she feels.
Cub #1 repeats what Cub #2 said.

Step 3 - Agree what the problem is and come up with some solutions.
Cubs #1 and Cub #2 agree on a solution.

Step 4 - Cubs agree to follow the solution they come up with. If you can't decide on a solution or have more problems, ask your leader to come up with some ideas.

6. Another way to solve pack problems is for all Cubs to work together to create a pack "Code of Conduct." Ask your leaders to help write down rules that you and the other Cubs think are fair and that everyone should follow while in the pack. Post these rules and try to follow them. And remember to follow your Cub Promise, Law, and Motto too!

If you are able to do some of these things, you'll help the pack a lot and you can be proud that you've done your best to make Cubbing better for all the Cubs and leaders.

If you are a sixer or a second, here are some other things you can do to help your pack.

1. Try to help your six get ready for each new activity. If Cubs need to take off or put on sashes, and neckerchiefs, have them do it as quickly as possible. Ask them to line up quietly and set the example by being quiet yourself.

2. A six box is a useful place to keep sashes, neckerchiefs, and Cub Books safe when you are not using them during the meeting. If your six doesn't have one, see if you can find a box you can use. You and the other Cubs in your six can decorate the box with your six colours.

3. Trying to boss Cubs around doesn't work very well. They'll listen to you much better if you're polite and friendly. Be a leader by sharing your experience and showing the way for younger Cubs to follow.

4. Many packs have a sixer's council where the sixers, and sometimes the seconds, meet with Akela and some of the other leaders. During the sixer's council, you can talk about things the pack might do and suggest ideas for activities you think might be fun. If your pack doesn't have a sixer's council, ask your leaders to think about starting one.

5. Try to hold meetings of your six to get ideas from your Cubs to pass on to your Akela or the sixer's council. Sometimes it's hard to find time for a six meeting, but you might ask your Cubs to come early every once in a while so you can meet before the opening Grand Howl. Or you can ask Akela to allow time for six meetings during the regular meeting. Six meetings can be very short; five or 10 minutes is plenty.

6. Some sixers phone their Cubs before the meeting every week to remind them to bring everything they need. It can be a lot of work, but the phoning will help your six be ready for every meeting. And you may have a Cub in your six who doesn't have many friends and hardly ever gets phone calls. If so, your phone call may be very important to that Cub.

12

267

7. If you have a Cub in your six who always seems to be causing trouble, try not to be too hard on that Cub. Consider that problems at school or at home may be causing the unhappiness or frustration. Instead of criticism or name calling, try understanding and help. Use the ALS method to see if you can solve some of the problems. Encouragement to "do your best" will be of great help as well.

Being a sixer or second is not always easy, and you may not be able to do all of these things as well as you'd like to. That's okay. If you do your best, you'll do some of them very well.

I remember helping _____.

(Cub's name)

This is what I did:

_____

_____

_____

When I was a Cub, I remember that

_____

(Cub's name)

helped me.

This is what the Cub did:

_____

_____

_____

Here are some of the things I did to help my pack:

_____

_____

_____

_____

12

269

CHAPTER 13

On To Scouts

hen you become 10 years old, it's time to start thinking about going up to Scouts. Scouts are like Cubs in some ways: they like fun and adventure, too!

As a Scout, you'll join a group like your six, called a patrol and learn to look after yourself. With the other members of your patrol, you'll learn how to camp in comfort and how to cook on a camp stove. You'll also learn how to carry everything you need in just one pack, how to deal with emergencies, and many other things. As well, you'll learn about personal fitness, safety, community service, and your role in Canadian society.

Scouts is a chance to work with a patrol to make more decisions on your own, and do projects that really interest you. Your Troop leader will help guide you and teach you the skills needed to take on bigger adventures than you've tried in Cubs.

Maybe you'll want to hike down a backwoods trail, try winter camping and sleep in the snow, or go on a canoe trip. You may get a chance to attend a jamboree, where you'll meet Scouts from other parts of Canada and sometimes other countries, too. There's a lot of action in Scouts, and you'll want to get in on it.

You may be a bit nervous about going up to Scouts, and you will want to find out as much about Scouts as you can before you join the troop. Ask Akela to invite the troop Scouter to a Cub meeting some evening to talk to you and the other older Cubs. Maybe the troop Scouter will invite you to visit the troop so that you can meet the Scouts and try some of the things they do.

Because it's always easier when a group of friends join Scouts together, talk to the other older Cubs about joining with you. Even if you join Scouts by yourself, you'll make new friends quickly.

13

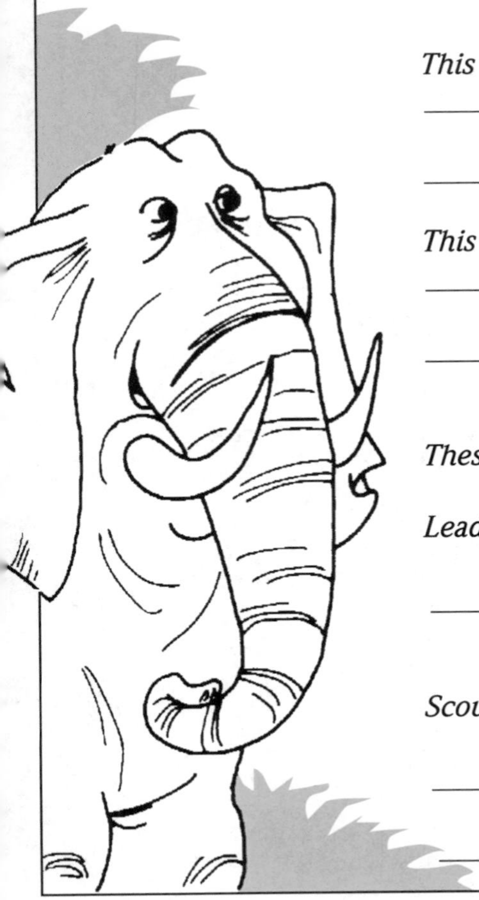

When I was still a Cub, I visited

_____
(name)

Troop on _____.
(date)

We did _____

_____

_____

This is what I liked best:

_____

_____

This is what I learned:

_____

_____

These are the new friends I met:

Leaders' names _____

_____

Scouts' names _____

_____

_____.

I went up to Scouts on

_____.

(date)

When you reach the end of your Cubbing days, look back and remember the fun you had and the things you learned. How about that favourite game that you wanted to play over and over again, or the time you got caught in the rain? What was your best outdoors experience? Of course, there may also have been times that weren't so much fun, but maybe you learned some things from them, too.

You know a whole lot more than you did when you joined Cubs and you learned a lot of those things in the pack. When you leave the pack to go up to Scouts or to do something else, you are going on to learn a lot more. You go with the best wishes of Akela and all your leaders.

Good luck and good hunting!

13

CHAPTER 14

My Wolf Cub Record

This was where my pack met:

_____

_____

_____

These were the Cubs in my six:

_____

_____

_____

_____

_____

_____

These were the other Cubs in my pack:

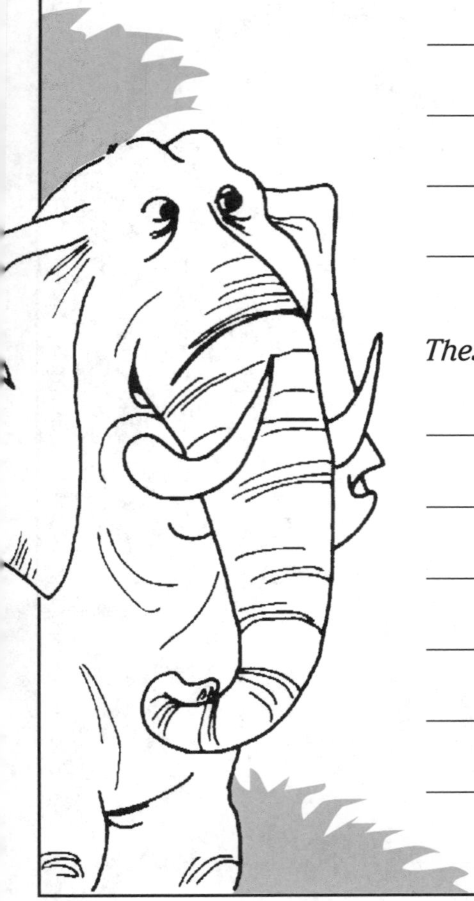

_____

_____

_____

_____

_____

_____

_____

These were the names of my leaders:

Akela _____

Raksha _____

Baloo _____

Bagheera _____

Chil _____

Kim _____

Others _____

Here are some of the things I remember best about being a Cub:

_____

_____

_____

_____

_____

_____

_____

_____

_____

Here are a few photos of my pack and some of the things we did.

Autograph Page

Notes

Index

Where to Find Things

SCOUTING AND THE FAMILY

A Grownup's Guide

To The

Wolf Cub Program

Welcome!

Thank you for registering your child in the Wolf Cub program. Cubbing offers an exciting variety of creative activities to spark any Cub's imagination. It also promotes wholesome personal development.

Scouts Canada believes that children learn by doing. Cub activities encourage children to discover and understand their world through play and adventure. Briefly, let's talk about how you and Scouting can work together to help your child do his or her best.

Scouts Canada And Your Child

Scouts Canada is the largest youth educational organization in Canada. With a quarter of a million members across the country, we also form part of the world-wide Scouting Movement which includes over 16 million members in 150 countries.

Scouting runs youth programs specifically designed for each age grouping: Beavers (5-7 years old), Wolf Cubs (8-10 years old), Scouts (11-14 years old), Venturers (15-17 years old), and Rovers (18-26 years old).

To understand how Cubs can meet your child's needs, let's look at what makes Scouting special.

Scouts Canada's Principles

Scouting is based on three broad principles which represent its fundamental beliefs.

Duty to God: This is defined as: "Adherence to spiritual principles, loyalty to the religion that expresses them and acceptance of the duties resulting therefrom."

Duty to Others: This is defined as: "Loyalty to one's country in harmony with the promotion of local, national and international peace, understanding and cooperation", and "Participation in the development of society, with recognition and respect for the dignity of one's fellow-being and for the integrity of the natural world."

Duty to Self: This is defined as: "Responsibility for the development of oneself." This is in harmony with the educational purpose of the Scout Movement whose aim is to assist young people in the full development of their potentials.

Scouting's core philosophy and values are expressed by the principles. These form a "code of ethics" for how Scouting expects all members to conduct themselves while participating in activities.

The Wolf Cub promise, law and motto are age-appropriate versions of Scouting's principles.

Wolf Cub Promise, Law And Motto

Promise
> I promise to do my best
> To love and serve God, to do my duty to the Queen;
> To keep the law of the Wolf Cub pack,
> And to do a good turn for somebody every day.

Law
(i) The Cub respects the Old Wolf *,
(ii) The Cub respects himself/herself.
    *(an "Old Wolf" refers to a leader or any respected adult)

Motto: Do Your Best

Scouts Canada's Mission

Scouting's principles are put into action and focus through our mission statement. Scouting's mission is:

> "The mission of Scouting is to contribute to the education of young people, through a value system based on the Scout Promise and Law, to help build a better world where people are self-fulfilled as individuals and play a constructive role in society."

Scouting's mission seeks to help develop the whole child. While some children may excel in school or when playing sports, to fit into society a person must be well-rounded mentally, physically, socially and spiritually to the best of their ability.

Cub Program Goals

In order to fulfil Scouting's principles and mission, the Cub program is geared specifically to meet the developmental needs of most 8-10 year olds. The program emphasizes activities which encourage Cubs to:

- express and respond to God's love in their daily lives
- do their best
- keep fit
- satisfy their curiosity and need for adventure and new experiences
- be creative and develop a sense of accomplishment
- make choices
- develop a sense of fair play, trust and caring
- work together in small groups and experience being a leader
- participate in outdoor activities
- learn about the natural world and their part in it.

In Wolf Cubs, "Do Your Best" nicely sums up the approach to activities described in this book. Cubs need adult support and approval as they play, learn and discover. Children need this for building self-esteem and self-confidence. It is critical for them to feel a sense of accomplishment for what they did, rather than being taught that only winning counts. Scouting believes that Cubs who "do their best" in any activity deserve equal recognition and praise.

How Packs Are Organized

The Wolf Cub theme is based on Rudyard Kipling's *The Jungle Book*. It provides a sense of outdoor adventure and fantasy that appeals to a Cub's imaginative mind. The "pack" refers to all members in your child's Cub program. Within the pack, Cubs are broken into small groups called "sixes". A Cub who is asked to lead a "six" is called a "sixer". The Sixer has an assistant called a "second". Cubs usually rotate through these early leadership jobs based on age and experience.

The primary adult leader of the pack is referred to as "Akela" — the name of the old wolf and leader of the pack in *The Jungle Book*. Other leaders take a "jungle name" such as Baloo (the bear), or Bagheera (the panther). Your pack may also have a "Kim" — a Scout who works with the Cubs. Kim is another Kipling character. Older Cubs are sometimes invited to work with a Beaver colony. Each Cub helper working in a colony is called "Keeo", after a character in the Beaver book *Friends of the Forest*.

The leaders in your Cub's pack are supported by a group committee. The committee is responsible for ensuring the programs offered meet Scouts Canada's guidelines and that the pack has enough resources to operate effectively. The group committee represents a sponsor which is the overall partner with Scouts Canada. Sponsors are typically community centres, clubs, religious institutions or parent groups. The sponsor works closely with Scouts Canada to ensure Scouting programs and resources are meeting the needs of all its youth and adult members.

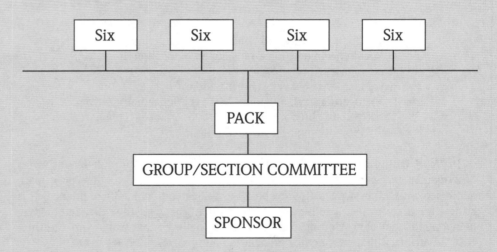

After learning a bit about Cubs, your child will be ready to become "invested", or formally welcomed, into the pack. You will be invited to attend the "investiture ceremony" to help welcome your child into the Cub pack.

Your Role in Cubbing

Scouting is a family-based organization. Activities we offer, plus the values and skills we provide, are aimed at supporting your efforts to teach your child what is needed to become a well-rounded person. Your personal involvement is important to help reinforce the lessons your Cub learns. Here are some suggestions to help you become involved:

- Sit down with your child and look through the *Cub Book* together. What activities do you find interesting or appealing? How could you work on these activities as a family?
- Find out what activities leaders plan to run in your child's pack. Most leaders set aside time at the first meeting to ask Cubs what they would like to do. They draw up program plans from the children's input.
- Get to know leaders by their real names. Too often parents only know leaders by their "jungle" names. Leaders are truly interested in your child's welfare. Tell them what your child likes to do. This will help them plan fun activities.
- If your Cub is interested in working on an activity outside of the meeting, or you want to make it a family project, talk over your plans with the leaders. They can provide useful tips and tell you how well it fits into the weekly programs.
- Your talents, hobbies and interests are great program assets worth sharing with children. Find out how you can become a resource for the pack's programs. This will let you spend valuable time with your child and share experience. Cubs really enjoy showing off for an adult family member who attends a meeting. This sense of pride helps strengthen adult-child relations. When your child joins Cubs, you become part of the pack's support team.
- Become a leader. Scouts Canada offers up-to-date training and resource materials. Leadership is fun and exciting. You will be with your Cub during a special time and see him (or her) develop and grow before your eyes. As well, the friendship and camaraderie you'll share with other parents can lead to long-lasting relationships and memories.

Helping Cubs Stay Safe And Healthy

A child's health and safety are the most important issues facing any parent. The world is quickly changing and the stress on today's Cub is growing daily. The Wolf Cub program has specific activities which help a child explore important social issues, such as alcohol and drug abuse, smoking and personal safety. Take the opportunity to discuss these issues openly. It is a perfect chance to share your insights, values and experience with your child.

Now that you have been introduced to Wolf Cubs, take a few minutes to leaf through the *Cub Book*. You'll notice that there are six activity areas. While your Cub will only see the fun and excitement the activities present, each area focuses on a clear purpose and goal. The purpose and goals for each activity area set out how the activities are relevant to today's child while meeting their developmental needs.

THE NATURAL WORLD ACTIVITY AREA

Purpose: To create a feeling of care and concern for the natural world and an interest in nature study.

Goals:
- To provide practical environmental activities that explore the wonders of nature.
- To develop an understanding that all life requires food, water, shelter and space.
- To explore and develop an understanding of the positive and negative impacts people have on the environment.
- To give direct ideas on how to help the environment in everyday situations.

THE OUTDOOR ACTIVITY AREA

Purpose: To provide opportunities for Cubs to develop self-confidence and early leadership skills through the introduction of basic camping and other outdoor pursuits.

Goals:
- To instruct Cubs on how to enjoy the outdoors safely.
- To introduce Cubs to various outdoor pursuits through age-appropriate activities based on simple skill learning and fun.

THE CREATIVE EXPRESSION ACTIVITY AREA

Purpose: To encourage Cubs to creatively explore and express themselves through activities which utilize imagination and innovation.

Goals:
- To develop a creative outlet for child interests through the use of music, arts, and crafts in the Cub program.
- To enhance Cub awareness of how modern technology can be used for creative expression.
- To stimulate and foster Cub literacy through activities which promote, or require, reading skills.
- To provide opportunities for Cubs to pursue a project from start to finish, thereby producing a sense of accomplishment.

THE HEALTH AND FITNESS ACTIVITY AREA

Purpose: To encourage Cubs to lead active and healthy lives and to have a positive image of themselves.

Goals:
- To encourage Cubs to have healthy lifestyle attitudes through developing active living habits.
- To promote the positive benefits of being involved in physical activities.
- To educate Cubs about health risks associated with tobacco products.
- To educate Cubs about health risks associated with drug and alcohol abuse.
- To encourage the practice of good hygiene habits for maintaining personal health and promoting self-reliance.

THE HOME AND COMMUNITY ACTIVITY AREA

Purpose: To create in a Cub a positive feeling of family and community responsibility, as well as personal self-reliance through opportunities to develop home care skills and knowledge about various community services.

Goals:
- To provide support to the Cub's family by teaching skills related to home care, safety and maintenance.
- To explore and appreciate the challenges facing disabled people in the community.
- To explore what services are needed to support a community, and how a person would access these services if required.

CANADA AND THE WORLD ACTIVITY AREA

Purpose: To provide opportunities for Cubs to better understand how to actively participate in Canadian society and the world we live in.

Goals:
- To learn about and appreciate Canadian society through active participation in community service projects.
- To discover and learn about their own faith and the various world religions.
- To participate in programs which highlight people and their cultures that make up Canada and the world.
- To demonstrate the inter-relationships Canadians have with people in other countries.

WOLF CUB SPECIALTY BADGES

Purpose: To provide flexibility in the Cub Program.

Goals:
- To provide a way to recognize a Cub who has a special interest.
- To provide a way to recognize a pack that has a special interest.

Get involved and participate in your child's Cubbing experience.
You'll be glad you did.

WOLF CUB ACTIVITY AREA ACHIEVEMENT CHART

NATURAL WORLD	OUTDOOR ACTIVITES	CREATIVE EXPRESSION	HEALTH AND FITNESS	HOME AND COMMUNITY	CANADA AND THE WORLD	SPECIALTY AREAS
BLACK STAR	GREEN STAR	TAWNY STAR	RED STAR	BLUE STAR	PURPLE STAR	(N/A)
BADGES Astronomer Gardener Naturalist Observer Recycling World Conservation	**BADGES** Camping Cooking Fishing Hiking Trailcraft Watercraft Winter Cubbing	**BADGES** Artist Carpenter Collector Computer Entertainer Handicraft Musician Photographer Reader	**BADGES** Athlete Cyclist Skater Skier Snowboarder Swimmer Team Player	**BADGES** Disability Awareness Family Helper Family Safety First Aider Guide Home Repair Law Awareness Pet Care	**BADGES** Aboriginal Awareness Canadian Heritage International Trade Space Exploration World Cubbing World Religions Language Strip Religion in Life	**BADGES** Individual Specialty Pack Specialty
AWARD Canadian Wilderness	**AWARD** Canadian Camper Canadian Heritage Trails	**AWARD** Canadian Arts	**AWARD** Canadian Healthy Living	**AWARD** Canadian Family Care	**AWARD** World Citizen	(N/A)

Wolf Cub Program Evaluation

We would like to hear your ideas and suggestions on how to make the Wolf Cub program better. Please send your comments to:

> Scouts Canada – Wolf Cubs
> 1345 Baseline Road
> Ottawa, ON
> K2C 0A7
>
> or email us at:
> mailbox@scouts.ca

Please include your name and address if you wish us to write back to you.

 Notes